Test Your English Vocabulary in Use

Elementary

SECOND EDITION

Michael McCarthy
Felicity O'Dell

CAMBRIDGE
UNIVERSITY PRESS

CAMBRIDGE UNIVERSITY PRESS
Cambridge, New York, Melbourne, Madrid, Cape Town, Singapore,
São Paulo, Delhi, Dubai, Tokyo

Cambridge University Press
The Edinburgh Building, Cambridge CB2 8RU, UK

www.cambridge.org
Information on this title: www.cambridge.org/9780521136211

First published 2010

Produced by Kamae Design, Oxford

Printed in the United Kingdom at the University Press, Cambridge

A catalogue record for this publication is available from the British Library

ISBN 978-0-521-13620-4 Edition with answers and CD-ROM
ISBN 978-0-521-13617-4 Edition with answers
ISBN 978-0-521-13619-8 Edition without answers
ISBN 978-0-521-13621-1 Test Your English Vocabulary in Use Elementary

Contents

Everyday verbs

Words and grammar

Thanks and acknowledgements

Many thanks are due to the editorial team under Nóirín Burke at Cambridge University Press who steered this book through the preparation of this new edition. We are particularly grateful to Caroline Thiriau, Hazel Meek, Emily Hird and Janet Weller, who have provided us help and guidance in the production of these tests. Thanks are also due to Jeanette Alfoldi and the production team, and Kevin Doherty for the proofreading.

Michael McCarthy
Felicity O'Dell
Cambridge, October 2009

Introduction

Who is this book for?

Test Your English Vocabulary in Use (Elementary) aims to help students check their vocabulary learning. It can be used by all elementary learners of English who want to test their vocabulary. It will also be useful for learners who are using *English Vocabulary in Use (Elementary)* and want to test their progress. Learners can use this test book alone, but the tests can also be used by a teacher working with groups of students.

How is the book organised?

The tests correspond in focus to the 60 units of *English Vocabulary in Use (Elementary)*. The Contents page shows you how the tests are grouped by category. Every test is independent and you do not need to do the tests in a particular order, as they do not become progressively more difficult.
Each test has a total of 30 marks, and the number of marks for the exercises is given within each test. There is an Answer key at the back of the book. A list of phonemic symbols is given on page 94.
Also at the back of the book, you will find a Personal diary. Here, you can make a note of the words you found difficult to remember.

How do I use this book?

If you are working alone with this book, first look at the Contents page, and choose the tests that interest you. You will find different types of vocabulary tests, such as tests on everyday verbs, tests on words and grammar, tests on different topic areas. Try to do different kinds of tests to give you variety. Remember, you do not need to do the tests in a particular order.
If you are using *English Vocabulary in Use (Elementary)*, you can use the tests after finishing a unit from the book. You can do this immediately after finishing a unit, or wait a while (e.g. a week) and use the test as a revision exercise.
You can use the tests more than once by writing the answers in pencil and rubbing them out when you have checked your answers. Alternatively, you could write your answers on a separate sheet of paper.
When you have checked your answers, you could write any words you had problems with in your Personal diary.

The marking scheme

You will find notes on the marking scheme at the beginning of the Answer key on page 67. The marking scheme is just to give you an idea of how well you know the vocabulary, but you do not have to use this marking scheme if you do not want to.

The family

1.1
10 marks

Complete these sentences.

Example: I'm his sister – he's my .....brother.......................... .

1 I'm her father – she's my ....
2 He's my mother's brother – he's my ....
3 I'm his mother – he's my ....
4 He's my brother – I'm his ....
5 I'm his daughter – he's my..................................... .
6 She's my mother – she's my son's ....
7 He's my son – he's my mother's ....
8 He's my father – he's my daughter's ....
9 She's my mother's sister – she's my ....
10 They're my father's mother and father – they're my ....

1.2
10 marks

Complete the crossword.

Across

1 If you had only one child, would you like a son
   or a .... ?
4 Your uncle's son.
7 Mother and father together.
8 Do you .... from a big family?
10 Have you got .... brothers or sisters?

Down

2 Your mother's brother.
3 Your brother's son.
5 Girl with the same parents as you.
6 Your brother's daughters.
9 A person with no brothers and sisters is an
   .... child.

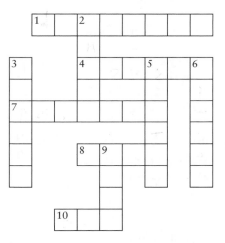

1.3
10 marks

Are these statements correct? Circle the correct answer and correct any wrong sentences.

1 My nephew John is my mother's sister's husband.   YES   NO
2 My grandfather is my father's father.   YES   NO
3 Mary and David are married. Mary is David's husband. YES   NO
4 I'm Philip, this is Nellie. We're married. She's my wife. YES NO
5 We talk about two wifes and two childs.   YES   NO

Birth, marriage and death

2.1
10 marks

Circle the correct <u>underlined</u> word.

Example: Bill <u>is</u> / (was) born in London in 1972.

1 My parents <u>are/were</u> both born in Scotland in 1960.
2 Kay <u>got/went</u> married <u>to/with</u> Ben last year.
3 After they got married they went on their <u>wedding/honeymoon</u> to Italy.
4 My grandparents were <u>marry/married</u> for 40 years.
5 His grandfather <u>dead/died</u> ten years ago.
6 He died <u>of/with</u> a heart attack on his 100th birthday.
7 They are going to <u>call/called</u> the baby Emily <u>from/after</u> her grandmother.
8 The old man became <u>ill/dead</u> last Sunday.

2.2
4 marks

Look at this form. What is the marital status of the people below?

1 Peter's wife died last year.
   He is ....
2 Anna has a husband.
   She is ....
3 Polly's marriage has broken up.
   She is ....
4 Jim does not have a wife.
   He is ....

Application form

What is your marital status?
Tick the correct box.

single ☐   married ☐
widowed ☐   divorced ☐

2.3
6 marks

Answer these questions about the picture.

1 What are the couple doing?   They are ....
2 What does the picture show?   A ....
3 What is the word for the special holiday they will go on after this day?
   The ....

2.4
10 marks

Complete these dialogues.

Example: A: Are you married?
              B: Yes.
              A: How long *have you been married?*
              B: Ten years already. I can't believe it!

1 A: Clare had a baby boy yesterday.
   B: How .... ?
   A: 3 kilos.
   B: What are .... ?
   A: Simon, I think. After Clare's father.

2 A: Jo's uncle is dead.
   B: Oh, I didn't know. When did he die?
   A: Yesterday.
   B: What .... ?
   A: He had a heart <u>attack</u>, I think.
   B: When is the .... ? I'd like to be there.
   A: It's on Thursday at 10.00 am.

3 A: Did you enjoy the wedding?
   B: Yes, it was great.
   A: Where did they go .... ?
   B: To France. They said it was fantastic.

Your score
/30

3.1

10 marks

First write the names of the body parts beside the picture. Then find these parts of the body in the word square.

Example: tooth

A	T	M	T	O	O	T	H
S	H	O	U	L	D	E	R
T	U	U	N	E	C	K	F
O	M	T	N	M	O	M	I
M	B	H	O	P	A	R	N
A	G	E	S	A	L	E	G
C	A	R	E	K	N	E	E
H	E	A	R	T	I	P	R

3.2

14 marks

Answer these questions about the body.

Example: What do we have ten of on our feet? toes

1 What do you see with and what do you hear with?
2 What two parts of your body do you regularly cut?
3 Which two parts of the body do you need to measure before you buy a man's shirt?
4 What two parts of the body do you need to measure before you buy or make a woman's skirt?
5 What does the heart move round the body?
6 What part of the body controls what you do?
7 What covers all your body?
8 On your foot you have a big toe. What do you have on your hand?
9 What part of the body do people often lie on when they sleep?
10 Is the 'ch' sound at the end of the word *stomach* pronounced like 'ch' in *church* or in *chemist*?

3.3

6 marks

Correct these sentences.

Example: John raised the weights above his bust.

John raised the weights above his chest.

1 Her hairs are black.
2 Paul has a pain in the side.
3 John has broken two tooths.
4 Please wash the hands before dinner.
5 My foots hurt.
6 The children put the hands up when they want to ask a question.

4 Clothes

4.1
12 marks

Write the correct word under each picture.

skirt belt boots trainers socks coat hat T-shirt scarf gloves tie shirt

1
2
3
4

5
6
7
8

9
10
11
12

4.2
5 marks

Underline the word on the right which has the same vowel sound as the word on the left.

Example: shirt   red/girl/here

1 tie   tea/hear/why
2 gloves   got/run/road
3 coat   note/not/hat
4 boots   foot/boat/suit
5 scarf   off/half/at

4.3
5 marks

Which five of these clothes words must always be used in the plural?

dresses hats trousers jackets tights jeans sweaters shorts shoes sunglasses

4.4
8 marks

Answer the questions.

1 Do you get dressed when you go to bed or when you get up?
2 What can you wear on your finger to show that you are married?
3 Who normally wears a dress – a man or a woman?
4 What do you call a jacket and trousers which you wear together?
5 What is another word for *sweater*?
6 Which is correct: 'Robert is wearing an umbrella / is carrying an umbrella / has an umbrella on'?
7 Which is correct: 'Lisa is using a skirt / Lisa has put a skirt on'?
8 What is another way of saying 'At night, I take my clothes off and go to bed'?

Your score
/30

5.1
10 marks

Put the words in the box into the correct column. Some words can go in more than one column.

~~blue~~ tall fair thin long slim green short brown dark fat

Eyes	Skin	Hair	Height and weight
blue			

5.2
10 marks

Answer these questions using the opposites.

Example: Is your cat old? No, she's young.

1 Has your sister got long, fair hair?
2 Is your aunt short and overweight?
3 Is your dog young?
4 Is your uncle ugly?
5 Has your mother got blonde hair?
6 Is your brother thin?
7 Is your little sister beautiful?
8 Is your cousin tall?

5.3
5 marks

Complete the five sentences describing this man.

Example: He's got brown/dark............. eyes.

1 He's got a ....
2 He's also got a ....
3 His skin is ....
4 He's got .... hair.
5 He is ....

5.4
5 marks

Make questions to match the answers on the right, using the words in brackets.

Example: (your sister / old / ?) How old is your sister? She's 14.

1 (you / tall / ?) .... 1 metre 56.
2 (the baby / heavy / ?) .... Nearly 5 kilos.
3 (the child / weigh / ?) .... Twenty kilos.
4 (your new teacher / look like / ?) .... She's tall and slim.
5 (her hair / colour / ?) .... Blonde.

Health and illness

6.1
10 marks

Match the sentences on the left with the sentences on the right.

1 I feel sick.
2 I'm fine.
3 I've got toothache.
4 I feel really ill.
5 I don't feel very well.

3 a I'm going to ring the dentist.
4 b I think I should call a doctor.
5 c I think I'll go home and rest.
1 d I think I ate something bad.
2 e I feel very well.

6.2
5 marks

Say the words aloud, then write them down.

Example: /ˈdɒktə/ doctor..............

1 /ˈhedeɪk/ ....
2 /məˈleəriə/ ....
3 /ˈæsmə/ ....
4 /ˈkænsə/ ....
5 /ˈkɒlərə/ ....

6.3
5 marks

Match the sentences below with the illnesses from 6.2.

1 Bad drinking water can cause it.
2 This makes it hard to breathe.
3 Smoking can cause it.
4 It's difficult to study when you have one.
5 You can get it from a mosquito bite.

6.4
10 marks

Fill the gaps.

1 I often feel s............................ in my job, so when I get home, I try to r............................ and not think about work.
2 My uncle Tim had a heart a............................ and he's in h............................ .
3 Every summer I get h............................ ; the flowers and grass make me s............................ .
4 I try to have a good, healthy d............................ with lots of fruit and vegetables.
5 E............................ is very important, for example, jogging, swimming, cycling.
6 If you've got a c............................d it's a good idea to stay at home and go to bed with a hot drink.
7 If you have a headache it may help if you take an a............................

Your score
/30

Feelings

7.1
10 marks

How do you feel? Choose the best word from the box.

Example: You've just had a long holiday with lots of good food and exercise.

You feel well.

angry cold happy hot hungry ill sad surprised thirsty tired ~~well~~

1 You haven't eaten for ten hours.
2 You went to bed at 2 am and got up at 6 am.
3 Someone has just broken a window in your new car.
4 It is a hot day and you haven't had anything to drink for three hours.
5 You have a very bad cold.
6 It is snowing and you do not have a coat with you.
7 You got very good marks in an important exam.
8 It is 35°C and you do not have air conditioning.
9 Your dog has just died.
10 You see your brother's photo on the front page of the newspaper.

7.2
4 marks

What are the opposites of these verbs and adjectives?

Example: good ....bad..........

1 love   2 cold   3 happy   4 ill

7.3
6 marks

Correct these sentences.

Example: Peter wants that his sister helps him.

Peter wants his sister to help him.

1 I like very much tennis.
2 I am very happy for your good exam results.
3 Jack hopes his girlfriend to phone him soon.
4 I like really ice cream.
5 My little sister prefers juice from milk.
6 Grandfather is little tired today.

7.4
10 marks

How do these people look? Use the letters to make a word and finish the sentence.

Example: Liz looks O T H.

Liz looks hot.

1 Bonnie looks T U S E P.
2 Colin looks G A R Y N.
3 Stan looks D A S.
4 Katie looks L I L.
5 Mark looks P E S S I D U R R.
6 Rob looks L C D O.
7 Nat looks D I R T E.
8 Clare looks P A P H Y.
9 Spot looks R I T T Y S H.
10 Fluffy looks G H U R Y N.

Conversations 1: Greetings and wishes

8.1

10 marks

What do you say?

1 You arrive at someone's office at 10 am. Good ....
2 You arrive at someone's house at 8 pm. Good ....
3 You lift your glass before starting a drink .... , everybody!
   with a group of people.
4 You want to get off a bus but there are .... , please.
   people in your way.
5 Someone sneezes. .... !

8.2

10 marks

Fill the gaps in the conversation with these phrases.

> Not too bad, thanks   Goodbye   And you   Hi   Congratulations
> How are you   see you soon   Happy birthday   good luck   Hello

RON: (1) .... , Fiona.
FIONA: (2) .... , Ron.
RON: (3) .... ?
FIONA: Fine, thanks. (4) .... ?
RON: (5) .... It's my birthday today.
FIONA: Oh! (6) .... !
RON: Thanks. So, how's university?
FIONA: Oh, great. In fact I just passed a big exam.
RON: Oh good! (7) .... !
FIONA: Thanks. The only problem is I've got another one next week.
RON: Really? Oh well, (8) .... !
FIONA: Thanks. Well, I must go now. Are you going to Anne's party on Saturday?
RON: Yeah. Well, (9) .... , then.
FIONA: Yes. (10) .... See you at the party.
RON: Bye.

8.3

10 marks

Correct the mistakes in these conversations.

1   LIM: Chinese New Year starts this week.
    DEREK: Oh really? Merry New Year!
2   DIANE: Here's the newspaper you asked me to get.
    NORBERT: Please.
    DIANE: No problem.
3   RUTH: This is my last day in the office till December 28th.
    WILL: Oh, well, I'll say Good Christmas, then.
    RUTH: Thanks. You too.
4   GEOFF: I swam a kilometre today.
    FRAN: Well made! You must be very fit.
    GEOFF: Yeah, I feel good.
5   BETH: It's my birthday today.
    SONYA: Oh, congratulations!
    BETH: Thank you.

Your score
/30

Conversations 2: Useful words and expressions

9.1 **Choose an expression from the box to fill each gap.**
10 marks

| ~~about~~ absolutely anyway around dear let's mind really up what why |

Example: ANNA: How ....*about*.......... doing something together this evening?
   ARI: Good idea. (1) .... don't we go to the cinema?
ANNA: Great. I'd (2) .... like that. Which film would you like to see?
   ARI: I don't (3) .... It's (4) .... to you.
ANNA: OK. (5) .... about that new one with Angelina Jolie? It sounds quite good.
   ARI: OK. (6) .... go and see that one, then. It starts at eight. I can come to your
     house at (7) .... seven and we can take the bus into town together.
ANNA: Well, let's just meet at the cinema. I'm going to be in town (8) .... –
     I have to go to the dentist at 5 o'clock.
   ARI: Oh (9) .... , I'm sorry! I hate going to the dentist, don't you?
ANNA: (10) .... !

9.2 **What do you say? Complete each expression in the speech bubbles. Then match them to**
10 marks **the correct pictures.**

Example:

It doesn't m_ _ _ _ _

Be c a r e f u l !

Well d_ _ _ !

What a p_ _ _ !

Hurry u_ !

Look o_ _ !

9.3 **Circle the correct underlined word.**
10 marks

Example: How around /(about) going out for a meal tonight?

1 What other/else do you want to do today?
2 JANE: Would you like some coffee? I haven't got any milk.
   NICOLA: It doesn't matter/mind. I prefer black coffee.
3 Other people in the class thought the test was difficult but I thought it was quite easy,
  absolutely/actually.
4 I don't / am not agree with your answer.
5 How about going/go for a swim?
6 The train arrived at up/around midday.
7 Let's meeting/meet at six.
8 They're really/absolutely nice people.
9 Look at/out! There's a banana skin on the floor!
10 Anyway/Else, let's get back to work now.

Food and drink

10.1
10 marks
Complete the two crosswords with the names of the fruit and vegetables in the pictures.

1

2

Down
1
2

Across
3
4
5

Across
1
2
3
4

Down
5

10.2
10 marks
Use the words from 10.1 to fill the gaps in the sentences. The first letter is given.

1 P............................ have a very hard skin and are difficult to cut, but the fruit is delicious.
2 O............................ always make my eyes water when I peel them.
3 When t............................ are red, they are ready to eat.
4 A b............................ is a good, healthy snack; fruit is better for you than sweets.
5 We use p............................ to make chips.
6 P............................ grow on trees, and are ready to eat in the autumn.
7 Green b............................ are a popular vegetable and are very good for you.
8 O............................ are often used to make juice.
9 You don't have to cook c............................ . They are very nice to eat raw.
10 Red g............................ and green ones are both used to make wine.

10.3
10 marks
Complete the conversations, using words from the box. Use each word once only.

fish pasta pizza fruit juice wine garlic peas strawberries hamburgers hot-dogs

1   EDITH: Are you a vegetarian?
    SYLVIE: Not really. I don't eat meat but I do eat .... because we live near the sea.
2 CARMEN: Do they only sell beer in British pubs?
      JOE: No, they sell .... too, and non-alcoholic drinks such as ....
3   VERA: What types of fast food do you like?
    RITA: Oh, everything – .... , ... , ...
4   KIERA: What's your favourite fruit?
    DONNA: .... I just love them! Especially with cream or ice cream!
5 NURDAN: Are there any vegetables you don't like?
    JANE: I don't like .... It's too strong for me, and I don't like the smell.
6   HENRY: What shall we have with the fish? Potatoes?
    LISA: Mmm, I'd prefer .... or rice.
    HENRY: Okay, what about vegetables? There are some frozen .... in the freezer.
    LISA: Yes, fine.

Your score
/30

11.1 Complete the dialogue.

10 marks

MARY: I've got some tomatoes out of the ....*freezer*.......... . Where is the big

red 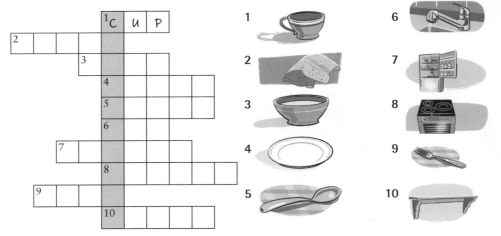 (1).............................. ? I want to make some soup.

JOHN: Look, it's in the (2).............................. under the (3).............................. .

MARY: Oh, so it is. Thanks. Now where's my favourite (4).............................. for cutting vegetables?

JOHN: It's right there in front of you. Between the (5).............................. and the (6).............................. .

MARY: Thanks. Let's have a (7).............................. of tea first.

JOHN: Good idea. I'll make it. Where's the (8).............................. ?

MARY: There, on the (9).............................. , next to the (10).............................. .

11.2 Use the picture clues to complete the crossword. The first one is done for you. What is

10 marks the word in the grey section?

	¹C	U	P
2			

1
2
3
4
5
6
7
8
9
10

11.3 Choose the right verbs from the box to complete these questions.

5 marks

find   go   ~~do~~   help   dry   have

Example: Would you like me to ....*do*.......... the washing-up?

1 Can I .... with the washing-up?
2 Where can I .... a cup?
3 Where do these knives .... ?
4 Shall I .... the glasses?
5 Do you .... a dishwasher?

11.4 Put the words together to make five compound nouns for things that you find in the kitchen.

5 marks *Example*: ....*teapot*..........

coffee   ~~tea~~   kitchen   liquid   maker   roll   tea   top   ~~pot~~   towel   washing-up   work

In the bedroom and bathroom

12.1
Match the words with the pictures.

| bedside table   wardrobe   chest of drawers   hairbrush   bed   dressing table |
| alarm clock   pyjamas   comb   bedside lamp |

12.2
Match the words with the explanations.

| bath   shampoo   toilet   towel   shelf   soap   shower   basin   razor   toothpaste |

1 You stand under it to wash.
2 You use it to shave.
3 You hold it in your hand when you wash.
4 You clean your teeth with it.
5 You can put things on it.
6 You fill it with water and sit in it.
7 You wash your hair with it.
8 Babies wear nappies before they learn to use this.
9 You dry yourself with it.
10 You can fill it with water to wash your hands.

12.3
Correct the mistakes. There are ten.

Every morning, when my alarm clock calls I awake up. Then I go up and do a shower and be dressed. I go downstairs and have breakfast. Then I go back to the bathroom and wash my teeth. At the end of the day, at about 11.30, I go upstairs, go undressed and go in bed. I listen to the radio for a while, then I turn the light and go to asleep.

Test 13 In the living room

13.1
10 marks

Choose words from the box to match the descriptions.

armchair   bookshelf   carpet   coffee table   curtains   light
light switch   ~~phone~~   remote control   sofa   TV

Example: You can talk to people on this.   .phone................

1 You sit on this. (2 words)
2 You walk on this.
3 You usually find books on this.
4 You can watch this.
5 You close these when it gets dark
6 You put this on when it gets dark.
7 You can turn the television on and off with this.
8 You turn the light off with this.
9 You can put drinks on this.

13.2
16 marks

Write the name beside each object, then read the text and draw a line from each object to the right place in the sitting room.

Example:

Look at this sitting room. The phone is on the armchair. There is a TV in the corner next to the door and the remote control is on the sofa. The picture is on the wall near the window and the hi-fi is next to the socket. The radio is on the bookshelf. There is a book on the rug and a lamp on the coffee table. There is a light switch on the wall next to the door.

13.3
4 marks

Complete each sentence with a verb.

Example: It's too dark in here. Could you ....switch........ the light ....on.......... , please?

1 It'll soon be dark. It's time to .... the curtains.
2 I'd like to talk to you. Can you .... the TV .... , please?
3 I always like to .... the news on TV.
4 When I want to .... after work, I lie on the sofa and listen to music.

Your score /30

14.1
10 marks
What do we call …

1 … a person who cuts your hair?
2 … a person who works in an office and writes letters, answers the phone, etc.?
3 … a person who lives in the country and grows food and/or keeps animals for food?
4 … a person you go to when you are ill, who examines you, decides what is wrong and gives you medicine?
5 … a person who designs and builds bridges, roads, etc.?
6 … a person who mends cars and other machines?
7 … a person who serves you in a restaurant?
8 … a person who cares for sick people in a hospital but is not a doctor?
9 … a person who gives you lessons?
10 … a person who works in a shop?

14.2
10 marks
Now use the words from 14.1 to fill the gaps. Use each word once only. Sometimes you will have to use the plural form.

1 The .... said it would cost €300 to fix my car.
2 I went for a walk in the countryside and met a .... looking after some sheep.
3 Do you like my hair? I have a new .... I think she's better than the old one.
4 Our .... said we're going to have a grammar test next Monday.
5 You can't talk to the director but you can leave a message with her ....
6 While I was studying I worked as a .... in a big store at weekends.
7 I like the idea of building big bridges and motorways, so I'd like to be an ....
8 To become a .... , you have to study medicine for five years.
9 The .... were very kind to me when I was in hospital. They were always there when I needed them.
10 The .... in that restaurant are very friendly.

14.3
10 marks
True or false? Write T for true, F for false. If you write F, say why.

1 A bus driver works in an office. ....
2 'What do you do?' is another way of saying 'What is your job?'. ....
3 A person who works in a bookshop is called a librarian. ....
4 A person who checks parked cars is called a traffic police. ....
5 If you do your job/profession in your own house or flat, you can say 'I work at home' or 'I work from home.' Both are correct. ....
6 It is correct to say 'I have an interesting work.' ....
7 A bank clerk works in a bank. ....
8 If someone asks you about your job, you can say 'I'm teacher.' ....
9 A person who repairs cars is called a mechanician. ....
10 Doctors and nurses work in hospitals. ....

Your score
/30

At school and university

15.1
10 marks

Which school subject is each person talking about?

Example: CARLOS: 'I need it because I want to study in Australia one day.' ....*English*............

1 MARK: 'It's my favourite subject because I love learning about other countries.'
2 SIMONE: 'I like it because I love drawing and painting pictures.'
3 KIM: 'I think it is very interesting to learn about animals and plants.'
4 TESSA: 'It's good because we run and jump and aren't sitting at a desk.'
5 ABDULLAH: 'Numbers are very interesting and I love working with them.'
6 ALEX: 'I love learning about how people lived in the past.'
7 DINA: 'I think it is very important to learn all about computers.'
8 MARIA: 'We study speed and light and movement – it's great.'
9 PAT: 'We learn songs and sometimes we can play instruments.'
10 MEENA: 'I enjoy doing experiments in the lab with different chemicals.'

15.2
10 marks

What are these things called? Put the letters in order to make words and then match the words with the pictures.

Example: ENP   *pen – a*

1 POH
2 RADOB
3 LURRE
4 KNOOTBEO
5 NPICLE
6 BURREB
7 TESACEST
8 GNARIWD IPN
9 CENOTIRADOB
10 PLINCE PHENARRES

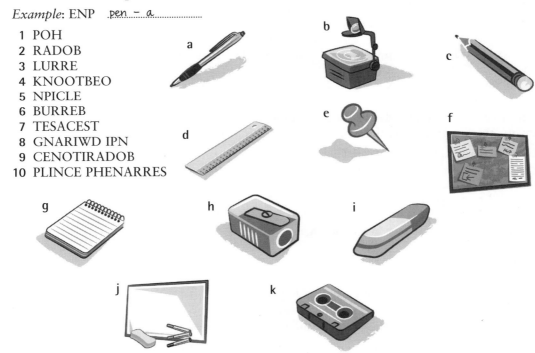

15.3
10 marks

Complete each sentence with a verb in the correct form (e.g. *get, got, getting*).

Example: At the end of a university course, you ....*get*............... a degree.

1 Mary likes school but she hates .... homework.
2 The children are .... their history textbook.
3 The teacher asked the children to .... a story about their favourite animal.
4 Children usually .... to ride a bike at the age of six or seven.
5 My brother is .... a course in computing this weekend.
6 When my English course .... I have to .... an exam.
7 Everyone hopes to .... their exams; no one wants to ....
8 Mr Jones .... my son history.

Your score
/30

16.1

6 marks

Here are six things we use to help us communicate. Put the letters in order to make words.

1 KYDBROAE   k......................................
2 TETERL   l......................................
3 LIEBOM HONEP   m................................... p...................................
4 TREELT BXO   l................................... b...................................
5 PONTELEHE   t......................................
6 CREESN   s......................................

16.2

10 marks

Fill the gaps in the conversations.

1   RORY: What's your a...................................... ?
   COLIN: It's 26 Park Road, Shilton, SH4 6BC.
2   TERRY: I'll ring you at ten o'clock tomorrow.
   MIKE: Okay, if I'm not at home leave a m...................................... on my answerphone.
3   ROB: How much was your camera?.
   NELL: It's about £200 in the shops. It's cheaper if you buy it o......................................
4   GARRY: How do I close this program?
   LINDA: Use the m...................................... to click on 'EXIT' in the top corner of the screen.
5   DANA: I want to save my work and take it to college tomorrow. Can you lend me a blank .... ?
   ANNE: Yes, sure, there's a box of them next to the computer.

16.3

10 marks

Put these sentences into the correct order to make a typical phone conversation. Write the numbers 1–10 next to the sentences.

He's not here right now. Who's calling?
Hello.
Okay, I'll tell him.
Hi, can I speak to Ken?
Bye.
It's Joanna. Could you give him a message?
No problem. Bye.
Yeah.
Thanks.
Could you tell him I called and I'll call back later.

16.4

4 marks

Write questions for these answers. Use the words in brackets.

1 They're on the memory stick on my desk. (our holiday photos)
2 It's Bob dot Jones at Freemail dot com. (email)
3 Yes, of course you can. The phone is in the kitchen. (make)
4 24th March. (date, letter)

Your score
/30

Holidays

17.1 **Answer these questions.**

10 marks

Example: What kind of sport is skiing?   ...*a winter sport*...

1 What kind of cheques can you use in any country?
2 What do you need to buy if you want to go on a bus, plane or train?
3 What are dollars, euros and yen examples of?
4 What do you call a holiday when you pay for everything (travel, hotel, etc.) together?
5 If a town has a lot of restaurants, discos and nightclubs, you can say that the
   .... is good.
6 What do you call all the things that you take with you on holiday?
7 What do you call a book that tells you lots of useful holiday expressions in another
   language?
8 What do people usually send their friends when they are on holiday?
9 What do you call the big bag you carry on your back on a walking holiday?
10 What kind of boat can you take your car on?

17.2 **Correct the mistakes in these sentences.**

5 marks

Example: Take your currency so you can take photos when you're on holiday.

   Take your camera so you can take photos when you're on holiday.

1 A coach is a large comfortable train.
2 When you go into another country, they look at your phrasebook.
3 You are only allowed to visit some countries if you have a special postcard.
4 A ferry takes you across land.
5 When you go on holiday, you put all the clothes and other things you need in a camera.

17.3 **Fill the gaps in this dialogue.**

15 marks

RICK: Have you been ....*on*.......... holiday this year yet, Meg?
MEG: Yes, we (1)........................... a fantastic holiday in Russia last month.
RICK: Great! How did you get there?
MEG: We (2)........................... from London to Finland and then we took a (3)........................... .
   across the Baltic Sea from Helsinki to St Petersburg. We spent a couple of days there and
   then we went to Moscow (4)........................... bus. We came home from Moscow
   (5)........................... train.
RICK: So, what was it like? What did you think of the local (6)........................... ?
MEG: It was delicious! And there was lots of excellent (7)........................... – very good
   discos and clubs, all open till very late.
RICK: Do you (8)........................... any Russian?
MEG: No, but we had a good (9)........................... and that helped us a lot. What about
   you, Rick?
RICK: We're (10)........................... on holiday next week. We're going to (11)...........................
   camping. We don't have to go to the airport to catch a (12)........................... – we're going
   in our own (13)........................... and we're staying in this country, so, of course, we can
   just use our ordinary money – we don't need to take any (14)........................... or foreign
   (15)........................... .
MEG: Well, I hope you have a wonderful time!

Your score
/30

Shops and shopping

18.1
8 marks
Which type of shop would you go to ...

1 ... to buy meat?
2 ... to buy bread and cakes?
3 ... to buy a present for someone?
4 ... to buy food and everyday things for your house?

5 ... to buy medicines and personal items?
6 ... to buy newspapers and magazines?
7 ... to buy stamps?
8 ... to buy books?

18.2
8 marks
Write the correct name for each department of a big store on the noticeboard.

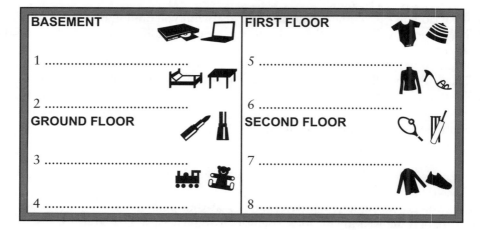

BASEMENT

1 ....

2 ....

GROUND FLOOR

3 ....

4 ....

FIRST FLOOR

5 ....

6 ....

SECOND FLOOR

7 ....

8 ....

18.3
12 marks
Fill the gaps in the conversations.

1 CUSTOMER: The .... said I could change it if I kept the
....

2 CUSTOMER: Where can I pay for this, please?
SHOP ASSISTANT: You can pay at that .... over there.

3 SHOP ASSISTANT: Can I .... you, madam?
CUSTOMER: Yes, how much does this hat .... ?
SHOP ASSISTANT: Oh, let's see. Here we are – €35.

4 (In a small café)
CUSTOMER: Can I pay by .... card?
WAITER: Sorry, sir, we don't have a machine.
CUSTOMER: Oh. Can I write a .... ?
WAITER: No, I'm sorry, sir, ... only. This is just a small café.

5 SALLY: I like this sweater. Shall I buy it?
MARY: Why don't you .... it on first and see how it looks on you?
SALLY: Yes, maybe I should.

6 (The customer has just bought a scarf)
SHOP ASSISTANT: There you are, madam. $25, and here's your .... , $5. Shall I
put it in a .... for you?
CUSTOMER: No thanks. I'll put it on. It's cold today!

7 CUSTOMER: I bought this jacket yesterday. It's too big for me. Do you have it in a smaller
.... ?

18.4
2 marks
Choose the correct sign to answer each question.

1 For which sign do you move your hand *away* from you?
2 For which sign do you move your hand *towards* you?

a   b

Your score
/30

In a hotel

19.1

Name these things.

Example: ....TV..............

1 ....

2 ....

3 ....

4 ....

5 ....

6 ....

7 ....

8 ....

9 ....

10 ....

19.2

Choose a verb from the box to complete these sentences.

Example: Could I ....exchange.......... some money, please?

| book order change check check out ~~exchange~~ fill in get have have sign |

1 I .... a reservation for a double room for tonight.
2 Please could you .... this form?
3 Please .... your name at the bottom of the form.
4 .... your bill carefully before you pay it.
5 Could I .... breakfast in my room, please?
6 To .... an outside line, you should dial 0.
7 I'd like to .... room service, please.
8 I would like to .... a room for next weekend, please.
9 Could I .... some dollars into euros, please?
10 We're ready to leave, so we'd like to .... now.

19.3

Answer these questions about staying in a hotel.

Example: What do you call the evening meal? ....dinner..........

1 What do you have to pay before you leave the hotel?
2 What do you probably need if your room is on the ninth floor?
3 What do you need to open your door?
4 What do you call a room for one person?
5 What do you call a room for two people?
6 If you phone Britain from another country, you must always dial 44 before the telephone number. What is the number 44 called?
7 What do you ask for if you want to wake up early in the morning?
8 Complete this sentence: 'I have a .... for a double room.' (The sentence means 'I have booked a double room.')
9 Where do you go when you first arrive at a hotel?
10 What do you ask for if you want to eat in your room?

Eating out

20.1
6 marks

Where would you hear these phrases? Match the phrases on the left with the places on the right.

1 A cheese sandwich to take to eat in the park, please.
2 A pint of lager, please.
3 Soup to start, then the chicken and mushrooms, please.
4 A burger, French fries and a coke, please, to eat here.
5 One coffee, one tea and two pieces of toast, please.
6 Where can I find knives and forks, please?

a café
b fast food restaurant
c self-service restaurant
d take-away
e pub/bar
f restaurant

20.2
20 marks

Fill the gaps.

1 At lunchtime I usually don't have a big meal; I just have a .... , for example a sandwich or some fruit.
2 If you order steak in a restaurant you can usually say if you want it .... , ... or well-... .
3 You don't have to have alcohol in a pub. They also have .... drinks like lemonade or coke.
4 If you want wine with your meal, you can ask the waiter for the wine ....
5 The restaurant has a tourist menu for only €20. You can choose from a list of .... , main courses and .... You can even have a .... meal if you don't eat meat.
6   WAITER: Are you ready to .... , madam?
   CUSTOMER: Yes. I'll have tomato salad to start, then the fish, please.

20.3
4 marks

Put the words into pairs. Use each word once only.

| potatoes | ~~green~~ | salmon | new | salad | apple | ~~beans~~ | pie | fruit | fillet |

Example: ...green beans.........

1 ....
2 ....
3 ....
4 ....

21.1
10 marks

What are these sports? Write questions, using either *play* or *go*.

Example:

Do you play football?

1 ....

6 ....

2 ....

7 ....

3 ....

8 ....

4 ....

9 ....

5 ....

10 ....

21.2
10 marks

Answer these questions.

1 If the sea is too cold, where can you go swimming?
2 What do you call the place where you play football?
3 What do you call the place where you play basketball?
4 Name a sport which needs snow.
5 Where can you do lots of different sports?
6 Name two sports which originally come from Japan. (2 marks)
7 Which sport has the Melbourne Cup?
8 Name one sport in which you can play 'doubles' (two players against two players).
9 Which sport has Formula One?

21.3
10 marks

Which word does not belong in each group? Explain why.

Example: football, baseball, table tennis, rugby

Table tennis – because all the others are played on a pitch.

1 swimming, skiing, sailing, kayaking
2 running, motor racing, horse racing, sailing
3 tennis, volleyball, badminton, baseball
4 basketball, table tennis, rugby, volleyball
5 tennis, volleyball, basketball, American football

our score
/30

Cinema

22.1
10 marks
Write the names of the types of films under the pictures. One of the types has two names.

thriller   cartoon   musical   romantic comedy   love story
comedy   action   horror   science fiction   western

1

....

2

....

3

....

4

....

5

....

6

....

7

....

8

....

9

....

22.2
12 marks
Correct the mistakes.

1 What's on the cinema this week?
2 At the weekends, we just relax and look DVDs.
3 I didn't like that film. I was boring.
4 Do you go to cinema very often?
5 It was a very funny film and I enjoyed very much.
6 I watched a good film in TV last night.

22.3
8 marks
Match the words and phrases below with one of the film types from 22.1.

1 'You are a British spy, Mr Bond!'
2 Donald Duck and Mickey Mouse
3 space rockets, men from Mars
4 These films make you laugh a lot.
5 'I love you; I've always loved you!'
6 Dracula, Frankenstein
7 guns, horses, men in big hats, North America
8 Sherlock Holmes, police, murder

Your score
/30

23.1
Are these statements true or false? If they are false, correct them.

Example: The dog is having a sleep.

<u>False – The dog is listening to the radio.</u>

1 The fair-haired woman is reading a newspaper. ....
2 The girl is talking on the phone. ....
3 The man with the beard is watching the news on TV. ....
4 The dark-haired woman is cooking. ....
5 The man without a beard is reading a magazine. ....
6 The boy is playing a computer game. ....

23.2
Choose verbs from the box to complete the conversation.

cook   download   grown   had   having   ~~playing~~   phone   stay   talk   use   watch

PAUL: Stop ....playing............ computer games, Anna. I want to talk to you. How about
        (1).. Sue and James around at the weekend?
ANNA: Good idea. It's a long time since we (2).. friends to dinner. I'll
        (3).. them now and ask them. Let's (4).. something
        special. They always make such delicious meals.
PAUL: Sure. Let's use some of the vegetables we've (5).. in the garden.
ANNA: Good idea. Do you want to (6).. the Internet tonight?
PAUL: No, I'd like to (7).. my new DVD. What are you going to do?
ANNA: I want to (8).. to my mother on the phone. I'd like to find out when
        she is going to come and (9).. with us. Then I want to
        (10).. some music.

23.3
Use the words below to make sentences.

Example: newspaper / a / day / I / every / read

<u>I read a newspaper every day.</u>

1 lunch / a / Grandfather / after / always / sleep / has
2 famous / reading / I / people / about / like / books
3 listen / I / the / my / car / radio / usually / in / to
4 films / favourite / musicals / My / are
5 a / has / My / of / lot / mother / novels

Music and musical instruments

24.1 Write the names of the musical instruments.
8 marks

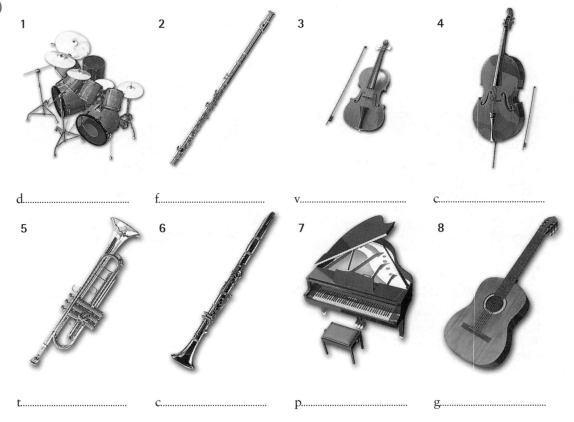

1

d.................................

2

f.................................

3

v.................................

4

c.................................

5

t.................................

6

c.................................

7

p.................................

8

g.................................

24.2 What do we call a person who ...
8 marks

1 ... plays the violin?
2 ... plays the flute?
3 ... plays the piano?
4 ... plays the trumpet?

24.3 Circle the correct underlined word.
10 marks

1 Mauricio likes <u>folk/folkloric</u> music.
2 I prefer <u>classic/classical</u> music.
3 This shop sells <u>music/musical</u> instruments.
4 I like all kinds of <u>music/musics</u>.
5 There was a very good <u>band / music band</u> at the festival.
6 I <u>don't/can't</u> stand jazz.
7 He is a professional <u>music/musician</u>.
8 My sister <u>learns/has</u> guitar lessons.
9 I like to <u>downplay/download</u> music from the Internet.
10 I prefer to listen <u>to/at</u> music in my room.

24.4 Unjumble the letters to make words connected with music.
4 marks

1 ZAZJ ....
2 REAPO ....
3 TROERCAHS ....
4 KROC ....

Your score
/30

Countries and nationalities

25.1 Which continents are these countries in?

0 marks

Example: Thailand   *Thailand is in Asia.*

| Brazil | Colombia | Egypt | Spain | India | Italy | New Zealand |
| Pakistan | South Africa | ~~Thailand~~ | USA |

25.2 Complete this table.

0 marks

Country	Adjective	Language
Argentina		
Canada		
China		
Germany		
Japan		
Morocco		
Peru		
Portugal		
Poland		
Thailand		
Tunisia		

25.3 Are these sentences true or false? If they are false, correct them.

0 marks

Example: Rome is the capital of Canada.

  False: Rome is the capital of Italy.

1 Ottawa is the capital of the USA. ....
2 Dublin is the capital of Australia. ....
3 Lima is the capital of Peru. ....
4 London is the capital of Sweden. ....
5 Madrid is the capital of Russia. ....
6 Pretoria is the capital of Korea. ....
7 Canberra is the capital of Austria. ....
8 Tokyo is the capital of Japan. ....
9 Wellington is the capital of Chile. ....
10 Washington DC is the capital of the USA. ....

26.1

10 marks

Match the weather words on the left with the sentences on the right.

1	rain	a	You can't see it but it makes things move about.
2	sun	b	It makes a very loud noise.
3	thunder	c	When light comes suddenly from the sky, often during a storm.
4	fog	d	It's yellow and makes you feel warm.
5	snow	e	Water falling from the sky.
6	lightning	f	These are sometimes big and white and can be seen in the sky.
7	clouds	g	It's a very strong wind.
8	wind	h	It's white and cold.
9	storm	i	It's a strong wind and heavy rain together.
10	hurricane	j	You can't see things in the distance.

26.2

10 marks

If the adjective form ends in 'y', write it in the box. If it does not, put an X in the box.

	Noun	Adjective
1	fog	
2	sun	
3	lightning	
4	thunder	
5	wind	
6	hurricane	
7	snow	
8	rain	
9	thunderstorm	
10	cloud	

26.3

10 marks

Correct the mistakes.

1 Yesterday was a sunshine day, but today it's cloudy.
2 It's snowing in New York and fogging in Chicago today.
3 It's very wet in the Sahara Desert. It hardly ever rains there.
4 We had a stormthunder last night. It woke me up.
5 It was raining and winding, so we stayed at home.

27.1
5 marks

Complete these questions and answers.

Example: Excuse me, I'm looking ....*for*.......... a post office.

1 No problem. There's one just over there on the other .... of the road.
2 Can you .... me the way to the nearest bank, please?
3 No problem. Take the number 20 bus and .... off at the third stop.
4 Is there a car park .... here?
5 Yes. Turn right here and it's about 500 metres down that road .... the left.

27.2
5 marks

What places do these pictures show?

Example:

..........*shop*.......... ....

.... c.................. m..................

27.3
0 marks

Which words match these definitions? The first letter of each word is given to help you.

Example: He or she keeps order on the streets. ..*(police officer)*..

1 Trains arrive and leave from here. (r.......................... s..........................)
2 You can buy stamps and send parcels and letters here.
   (p.......................... o..........................)
3 These words are on doors to show you the way in and the way out of a building or area.
   (E.......................... ; E..........................)
4 This notice shows you that a machine is not working. (O.......................... of
   o..........................)
5 Visitors to a place can find out here about hotels and special places to visit.
   (t.......................... i.......................... o..........................)
6 This notice means that people must not have a cigarette here. (N..........................
   S..........................)
7 This is a part of town where people can only go on foot.
   (p.......................... a..........................)
8 There are lots of different shops here. (s.......................... c..........................
9 Local government takes place here. (t.......................... h..........................)
10 You can leave your car here. (c.......................... p..........................)

In the countryside

28.1
10 marks
Match the words on the left with the definitions on the right.

1	farm	**a**	large area full of trees
2	lake	**b**	smaller than a town
3	mountain	**c**	small house in the country
4	village	**d**	large area of water
5	hill	**e**	smaller than a road, not for cars
6	forest	**f**	the Thames, the Amazon and the Nile are examples
7	path	**g**	place where people keep animals and grow food
8	field	**h**	there are a lot of these in the Alps and in the Himalayas
9	cottage	**i**	closed piece of land where animals live or people grow food
10	river	**j**	high ground, but not as high as the Alps or Himalayas

28.2
10 marks
Use the words from 28.1 to fill the gaps. Use each word once only. Sometimes you will have to use the plural form.

1 She lives in a small .... of about 500 people.
2 We got out of the car and walked along a .... by the river.
3 If we cut down more and more trees there will be no .... left in the world.
4 The .... goes through three countries and then into the Mediterranean Sea.
5 The town has .... all round it; some of them are 3,000 metres high.
6 They have a house near a .... and have a boat they can use on it.
7 He has a little .... in the country, where he spends the weekends.
8 There were some sheep in the .... , eating the grass.
9 I lived on a .... when I was a child. I loved the animals and the open air.
10 The east of England is good for cycling holidays because there are not many

....

28.3
10 marks
Correct the mistakes. There may be more than one in each sentence.

1 I love the nature, so when I finish my studies I'm going to work in a conservatory area in the countryside.
2 In the summer we go to the mountains for picnics; in the winter we go for ski.
3 At the weekends, I like to get out of the city and go for a walk in the nature.
4 There are some fantastic wildlifes in the national park.
5 He lives in a beautiful house in the mountain.
6 Athens is a country in the city of Greece.
7 Everest is the highest hill in the world.
8 We live in the countryside and go walk most weekends.

Your score
/30

Animals

29.1
0 marks

What are these animals?

Example:

sheep

1 ....

2 ....

3 ....

4 ....

5 ....

6 ....

7 ....

8 ....

9 ....

10 ....

29.2
0 marks

Which animal word matches these definitions?

Example: a young hen .... chick ....

1 a young horse
2 the meat from a hen
3 a place where you go to see lots of wild animals from different countries
4 young birds, tortoises and snakes are all born from these
5 we get this from sheep and use it to make warm clothes
6 the meat from a pig (2 words)
7 we drink this and also use it to make cheese and butter
8 a long thin animal with no legs
9 the skin of cows – we use it to make shoes and handbags

29.3
0 marks

Which word does not belong in each group? Explain.

Example: hen, monkey, parrot, chick

Monkey – because the others are all birds.

1 lion, tiger, horse, cat
2 elephant, giraffe, snake, cow
3 calf, lamb, sheep, piglet
4 fish, tortoise, dog, pig
5 beef, foal, ham, chicken

30.1 Write the type of transport under each picture.

10 marks

Example:

.......car....... 1 .... 2 .... 3 ....

4 .... 5 .... 6 .... 7 ....

8 .... 9 .... 10 ....

30.2 Answer the questions.

10 marks

1 You want to find out where a place is. What can you look at?
2 What do you need to show when you arrive in a new country?
3 In which part of the train can you buy food / have a meal?
4 A ticket from A to B and back again is a *return* ticket. What do we call a ticket from A to B only?
5 Who checks your suitcases and other bags when you arrive in a new country?
6 What word means 'suitcases and other bags'?
7 What can you look at to find the times of buses or trains?
8 You need a car for your holiday but don't want to use your own car. What can you do?
9 What type of card do you need to get on a plane?
10 What do you call the people who work on the plane and bring you meals, etc.?

30.3 Circle the correct answer.

10 marks

1 The plane   (a) grounded   (b) took down   (c) landed   at 6.35.
2 I need to   (a) fill   (b) tank   (c) put   up my car. Is there a petrol station near here?
3 The train has just arrived   (a) by   (b) in   (c) at   platform number 5.
4 The officer   (a) controlled   (b) checked   (c) looked   my passport and said 'Welcome to Bolania.'
5 I'm going near your house. Can I give you a   (a) lift   (b) drive   (c) carry?

Your score
/30

UK culture

31.1
0 marks

Fill in the consonants to complete these names of special days.

Example: E A - - E - = *Easter*

1 - - - I - - - A -
2 - O - - I - E - I - - -
3 - E - - E A - ' - E - E
4 - A - - O - E'E -
5 - A - E - - I - E' - - A -

31.2
0 marks

Match a word on the left with a word on the right.

1 Christmas   Parliament
2 bank   eggs
3 Yorkshire   card
4 royal   tree
5 primary   family
6 roast   holiday
7 Prime   pudding
8 Easter   masala
9 Christmas   potatoes
10 Houses of   school
11 chicken tikka   Minister

31.3
5 marks

Put the words in the right column.

| bonfire | curry | fireworks | king | nursery | oven |
| Prime Minister | private | queen | secondary | state |

Types of school	Hot things	People
	bonfire	

31.4
5 marks

Answer these questions.

Example: On which special day do children get chocolate eggs? .... *Easter* ....

1 Which special day is on 14 February?
2 Which special day has bonfires and fireworks?
3 What kind of meat do people eat Yorkshire pudding with?
4 'Fish and *what?*' is a traditional British meal.
5 Which country did curry come to the UK from?

32.1 Complete the grey boxes in the chart.

10 marks

Crime	murder	mugging	3	car theft
Person	*Example:* murderer	mugger	terrorist	4 ....
Action	1 to .... somebody	2 to .... somebody	to attack somebody or a place for political reasons	5 to .... a car

Crime	6	shoplifting	9	drug dealing
Person	7	8	burglar	10 drug ....
Action	to rob somebody or a place (e.g. a bank)	steal things from a shop	to break into a house/flat	to sell drugs

32.2 Now use words from 32.1 to fill the gaps in these sentences.

12 marks

1 There was a .... in our street last night. Somebody .... into a house and .... a TV set, a DVD player and some cash.
2 Anna Frane's dead body was found in the river. She had been .... The .... was her ex-boyfriend.
3 .... is very easy in some shops, but many big stores have cameras to catch ....
4 The bank in the High Street was .... yesterday. The .... escaped in a blue sports car.
5 A student was .... as she was walking home. A young man took her money and credit cards.
6 A car .... took my car from the office car park. There have been three .... there this month.

32.3 True or false? Write T for true, F for false. If you write F, say why.

8 marks

1 If you are *innocent* you are not *guilty*. ....
2 If you do something wrong (e.g. park your car in a 'no parking' area) you have to pay a *find*. ....
3 Sometimes people break and destroy things (e.g. telephone boxes, trees in the park). We call the people who do this crime *vandalism*. ....
4 *Arrest* means that the police come and take somebody away because they think they are guilty of a crime. ....
5 We call violence and criminal actions at football matches *hooliganism*. ....
6 We call the place where people decide whether someone is guilty of a crime a *sentence*. ....
7 We call the place you have to stay in for many years if you are guilty of a bad crime a *prisoner*. ....
8 People who sell illegal drugs are called *drug dealers*. ....

Your score
/30

The media

Match the words on the left with the definitions on the right.

1	news	a	*The Simpsons* and *Mickey Mouse* are famous examples of this
2	soap	b	you can watch this at the cinema or on DVD
3	nature programme	c	regular programme about what is happening in the world
4	sports programme	d	programme which has interviews with famous people
5	talk show	e	programme about animals or plants
6	cartoon	f	programme about, for example, football or the Olympic Games
7	documentary	g	CNN, Eurosport, MTV and BBC1 are examples of this
8	film	h	TV programmes that show people living their lives, not actors acting
9	channel	i	magazine telling stories in pictures
10	reality TV	j	serious programme about society or nature
11	comic	k	TV serial that goes on for years about the lives of a group of people

Complete the crossword.

Example: 1 Our new ..*satellite dish*.. lets us get a lot more channels.

2 Mum's new .... has a great article on fashion.

3 She wants to be a .... and write articles for sports magazines.

4 When Pat won the tennis match he had to give an .... to the local paper.

5 The .... took notes during the football match and wrote his article later.

6 I like that .... – there are always interesting guests on it.

7 Buy the children a .... when you are at the newsagent's.

8 I mainly use my .... for going online.

9 I have to buy a .... every morning because I like to know what's going on.

10 Mum always watches her favourite Australian .... before the news.

11 This programme is boring. Let's try another ....

A satellite dish

Crossword answers spelling down: S A T E L L I T E D I S H

Which of these words go together with *newspaper* and which go together with *magazine*?

Example: ..news magazine..

women's   computer   ~~news~~   evening   teenage   morning

Problems at home and work

34.1
10 marks

Look at these pictures and choose a phrase to describe each one.

> It's not working.   It's dying.   He's cut his finger.   It's untidy.   It's broken.

1

2

3

4

5

34.2
10 marks

What could you do about the problems in 34.1?

1 What could you do to the man's finger?
2 What could you do to the cup or the TV? (2 different verbs)
3 What could you do to the desk?
4 What could you do to the plant?

34.3
10 marks

Fill the gaps. Use one word in each gap.

1 My computer .... yesterday, so I didn't get your email.
2 Our teacher was in a bad .... this morning, so the lesson was not very nice.
3 The ticket machine was out of .... , so I couldn't get a ticket.
4 I shouted at my sister. I must .... to her.
5 Jon and Sara have had a .... and are not speaking to each other.
6 I've .... my wallet. I must find it.
7 I can't find my credit card. Could you help me .... it?
8 The boss doesn't like it if my desk is .... and always asks me to
.... it.
9 There's a problem with my bike. Do you think you could .... it for me?

Your score
/30

Global problems

35.1 Look at the headlines. Which of the problems in the box will these articles be about?

10 marks

| car crash   earthquake   flood   forest fire   hurricane   pollution |
| snowstorm   strike   traffic jam   unemployed people   ~~war~~ |

Example:

BOMBS DESTROY ENEMY TANKS .... *war* ....

1 **WORKERS STOP WORKING AT CAR FACTORY**

6 **HOUSES UNDER WATER**

2 **CARS CANNOT MOVE IN CENTRAL LONDON**

7 **FISH DIE IN DIRTY RIVER**

8 **ACCIDENT ON MOTORWAY**

3 **STRONG WINDS DESTROY TOWN**

4 **HEAVY SNOW STOPS TRAINS**

9 **WORKERS LOSE THEIR JOBS**

5 **MORE TREES BURN IN AUSTRALIA**

10 **BUILDINGS FALL IN CALIFORNIA QUAKE**

35.2 Which word fills each gap?

10 marks

Example: The traffic j _ _ _ are very bad here in the mornings. .... *jams* ....

1 P _ _ _ people don't have much money.
2 U _ _ _ _ _ _ _ _ people don't have jobs.
3 H _ _ _ _ _ _ people don't have a place to live.
4 If the air is p _ _ _ _ _ _ _ , it is not clean.
5 If people are h _ _ _ _ _ , they want something to eat.
6 The busy time for traffic in the morning and evening is called the r _ _ _ h _ _ _ .
7 There were serious f _ _ _ _ _ last year after some very heavy rain.
8 The manager wouldn't agree to raise the workers' wages and so they decided to go o _
   s _ _ _ _ _ .
9 In summer there are a lot of tourists here and the town is very c _ _ _ _ _ _ .
10 The American W _ _ of Independence took place at the end of the eighteenth century.

35.3 Put the words in the box in pairs.

10 marks

Example: heavy rain..............

| air   car   cities   crash   crowded   earth   fire   forest   ~~heavy~~   homeless   hour   jam |
| people   pollution   quake   ~~rain~~   rush   snow   storm   strong   traffic   wind |

36.1
5 marks

What are these people doing? Write sentences using *have*.

Example: He's having a swim.

 1    2    3    4    5

....

36.2
5 marks

Match the phrases using *have* on the left with the explanations on the right.

1 have a game   a enjoy something
2 have a go   b be free to do something
3 have a good time   c try something
4 have a word with someone   d play something (e.g. tennis)
5 have the time to do something   e speak to someone

36.3
10 marks

Fill the gaps with the correct form of *have, have (got) to* or *have got*.

1 I asked for stamps in the shop but they .... any, so I
   .... go to the post office.
2 I .... a headache yesterday so I didn't go to class.
3 .... you .... a dictionary? Can I .... a look at it,
   please?
4 Everyone .... pay for the school trip seven days before
   we leave. That means we .... just three days before we
   .... pay.
5 Do you .... a moment? I'd like to ask you a question.
6 I .... my hair cut yesterday. Do you like it?

36.4
5 marks

What can you say using *have*? Choose a suitable expression for each situation.

> Can I have a go?   Can I have a word with you?   Have a good journey!
> Can I have a look?   Have a good time!

1 Someone is leaving for the airport to fly to New York.
2 Someone shows you a new mobile phone with the latest games on it.
3 Someone says they have lots of their holiday photographs on their mobile phone.
4 Someone is going out for the evening to a restaurant, then to a party.
5 You want to speak to someone about something important.

36.5
5 marks

Fill the gaps.

1 We had a .... in the new Chinese restaurant yesterday.
2 I have a .... with the boss at 10.30, but I can see you at 11 o'clock.
3 She has a violin .... with her new teacher at 5 pm today.
4 In our English classes, we have .... every day to do before the next lesson and
   we have an .... at the end of every term.

Your score
/30

Go / went / gone

37.1 Fill the gaps with the right word or words.

10 marks

Example: Let's go ....to......... the cinema this evening.

1 My mother goes to work .... bike.
2 The old lady went .... the house and .... the street.
3 Please go .... – I don't want you here!
4 Oliver went .... the stairs to his bedroom on the top floor.
5 In the morning I go .... to my office in the lift but at the end of the day I go
   .... the stairs.
6 I like to go to work .... car.
7 We've had a lovely holiday but we have to go .... home tomorrow.
8 Is this bus going .... the railway station?

37.2 Which meaning of *go* is used in each sentence? Write a, b or c next to each sentence.

5 marks
a move from one place to another   b do an activity   c talk about plans for the future

Example: I go to work by bike. ....*a*..........

1 Are you going to watch the football match tonight?
2 Larry goes to Paris on business every year.
3 I love going sightseeing when I'm on holiday.
4 What are you going to do next year?
5 Do you like going shopping?

37.3 Which activity is each person doing? Use an expression with *going*.

5 marks
Example:

Dan   1 Nora   2 Harry

Dan is going skiing.

3 Mel and Bob   4 Terry and   5 Nick
                                          Sarah

37.4 Look at Jim's diary. What is he going to do each day? Write ten sentences.

10 marks
Example:

On Monday Jim
is going to have
lunch with Mary.

30 Monday	Thursday **2**
Have lunch with Mary. Evening – meet Tom and Ricky.	Morning – go swimming. Evening – play table tennis with Mary.
31 Tuesday	Friday **3**
Visit grandmother.	Do some housework! Phone Aunt Sally.
1 Wednesday	Saturday **4**
Meet Pat for dinner.	Buy Tom's birthday present.
	Sunday **5**
	Give Tom his present. Take Mary to Tom's party.

WEEK **31**   W T F S S M T   M T W T F S S M T   W T F S S M T W T F
             1 2 3 4 5 6 7   8 9 10 11 12 13 14   15 16 17 18 19 20 21 22 23 24 25 26 27 28 29 30 31

38 Do / did / done

38.1

10 marks

Fill the gaps with the correct form: *do/does*, *did* or *done*. Two of the forms you need are negative.

1 MOTHER: Have you .... your homework?
    TOM: Yes, I .... it last night.
2 GERRY: .... your brother live at home with your parents now?
    LIAM: No, he .... , but my sister ....
3 PAUL: .... you like the concert yesterday?
    ULLA: Yes, I .... Why .... you go?
    PAUL: Oh, I had to study for my exam.
4 RITA: I feel really tired.
    DON: So .... I.
    RITA: We've .... a lot of work today.

38.2

5 marks

Write each sentence in another way, using *do*.

Sentence	Same sentence using *do*
Example: She's working in the garden.	She's doing the gardening.
1 What is your job?	
2 How do you spend the weekends?	
3 Let me wash the dishes.	
4 I always clean my house on Saturdays.	
5 I worked very hard but I failed the exam.	

38.3

15 marks

Correct the mistakes in these sentences.

1 MICHAEL: What does your father?
    JANE: He's a lorry driver. (1 mistake)
2 I don't like do homework but I know I have to do.
(2 mistakes)
3 He do a lot of business with companies in the USA nowadays. (1 mistake)
4 I saw her at the gym. She was done some exercises that looked very hard. (1 mistake)
5 DIANA: Liz, what you are do with all those clothes?
    LIZ: I do my washing. All my clothes are dirty.
(2 mistakes)
6 FATHER: Ivan, to do your homework now!
    IVAN: No. Not now. I do it later. Please, Dad!
    FATHER: No! I want you do it now! (3 mistakes)
7 MARIA: I does my best to learn all the new words every day.
    ANONA: So does I, but then I forget them again. (2 mistakes)
8 In our family, my father do the washing-up every day, my mother is do the gardening, but my brother never doing anything!
(3 mistakes)

Your score
/30

Make / made / made

39.1 **What is each person making? Write sentences.**

Example:

Ivan

Ivan is making a noise.

1 Pam

2 Tim

3 Rose

4 Chris

5 Isabelle

6 Phil

7 Sophie

8 Vincent

9 Katy

10 Nathan

10 marks

39.2 **Put these words in the right column.**

10 marks

lunch   your homework   a noise   an appointment   a mistake   some exercises the housework   the washing   an exam   a choice   the cooking

Do	Make
	lunch

39.3 **10 marks** **There are six mistakes in this letter. Correct them – the first one is done for you.**

Dear Jane,

I've had such a busy day. After school I ~~made~~ *did* my homework. I did it very quickly, so I think I probably did a lot of mistakes. Then my friend and I went to a film. The hero died, so it made us feel very happy. But it was a very long film, so it made I feel quite tired too. When I got home I had to make the washing. Then at last I could go to bed.

I've got to make an exam next week, but let's meet at the weekend.

Love,

Annie

Come / came / come

40.1
5 marks

What are the people saying? Fill the gaps, using expressions with *come*.

1

Hi, Mum! I've finished my shopping and I'm .... See you in 20 minutes.

2

Timmy, ... !
Don't stand there!

3

4

5

I'm sorry, madam, your jacket will not be ready till tomorrow.

Hi, Jane. I'm just .... the station. My train was late.

His name's Miguel and I think he .... Mexico.

Oh. Okay. I'll .... tomorrow.

40.2
5 marks

Match the underlined words on the left with the definitions on the right.

1 Jo is in hospital. Do you want to <u>come and see</u> her with me?
2 We're going to the park. Do you want to <u>come along</u>?
3 I <u>came across</u> an old photo of you yesterday.
4 <u>Come round</u> at about five o'clock and have a cup of tea.
5 Her name <u>came up</u> in conversation.

a found by chance
b go to someone's house
c visit a person or place
d was mentioned
e go with someone to a place

40.3
20 marks

Correct the mistakes in these conversations.

1 LORNA: Has your brother come back of Germany yet?
  JAMES: Yes, he came to home last Friday. (2 mistakes)
2 HILDA: Do you know Stockholm? I've never been there.
  RYAN: Yes, I came there last summer for a few days. (1 mistake)
3 STEVE: What nationality is Tanya? Where she comes from?
  FELIX: She's coming from Moscow. She's Russian. (2 mistakes)
4 ANNA: I was surprised to see Julia in your office.
  NANCY: Yes, she didn't even knock. She just came into. (1 mistake)
5 EVA: Do you know what the English word 'cabbage' means?
  PACO: Yes, it came upon in the lesson yesterday. It's a vegetable. (1 mistake)
6 ADA: Would you like to coming round to my house this evening to watch a DVD?
  NIK: Yes, but my cousin is staying with me. Can he come long?
  ADA: Of course. He can came too. (3 mistakes)

41.1 How long did it take people to do these things? Make sentences using *took*.

10 marks

Sam	8.00 – left home to go to work	8.30 – arrived at work

Example: It took Sam half an hour to go/get to work.

1 Miranda	7.30 – left home to go to work	8.30 – arrived at work
2 Tony	9.00 – started checking emails	9.20 – finished checking emails
3 Maggie	19.00 – started doing homework	20.15 – finished doing homework
4 Jeremy	10.00 – got on plane to fly to Paris	11.30 – arrived in Paris
5 Julia	12.45 – started eating lunch	12.55 – finished eating lunch
6 Mark	15.15 – started writing report	17.45 – finished writing report
7 Angela	18.25 – got on train to go to London	22.05 – arrived in London
8 Paul	10.00 – started repairing bike	13.30 – finished repairing bike
9 Rosemary	July 1 – started writing story	Sept 30 – finished writing story
10 Ken	December 2002– started writing poem	December 2010 – finished writing poem

41.2 Use the words below to write full sentences.

10 marks

Example: I / take / French course / last year.

   I took a French course last year.

1 I / take / train / when / go / airport / last summer
2 Anita / take / English exam / tomorrow
3 Kay / want / take / Greek lessons
4 Her father / take / bus / the office
5 Pete / take / underground / to work every day

41.3 Look at the pictures and write the English words beside them. Then choose the right
10 marks word to fill each gap in the sentences below.

a ....

b ....

c ....umbrella..............

d ....

e ....

f ....

Example: It's raining – take your ......umbrella...... with you.

1 You'll have time to read on the train, so don't forget to take a ....
2 You'll want something to eat, so take an .... with you.
3 You might want to take some photos, so do take your ....
4 Take some .... – you may want to buy some postcards.
5 It'll be cold in the evening – take a .... with you.

Your score /30

Bring / brought / brought

42.1
10 marks

Fill the gaps with the correct form of *take* or *bring*.

1 She often comes to see me and always .... me flowers.
2 I'm just .... this book back to the library. I'll be back in half an hour.
3 She borrowed my camera but she .... it back the next day.
4 Are you going to the kitchen? Will you .... me a glass of water?
5 .... this letter to the post office and post it for me, will you?

42.2
10 marks

What could you say? Use *take* or *bring* in your answer. There may be more than one possible answer.

1 Your friend has to catch a train. You have a car. Offer to drive them to the station.
2 A friend is going into town. You have a parcel which you want to post.
3 You're having a party at your house. One of your friends plays the guitar. Invite them with their guitar.
4 You've just bought a sweater but the size is wrong. Tell a friend what you're going to do when you go to town tomorrow.
5 A good friend is going to Belgium for a few days. You'd like some Belgian chocolates.

42.3
10 marks

Correct five mistakes in these emails.

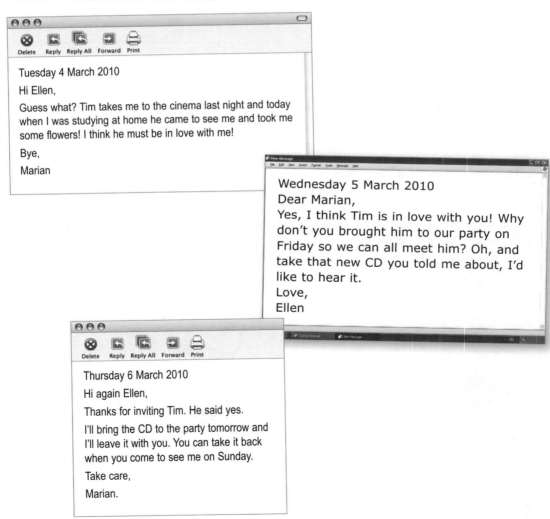

Tuesday 4 March 2010

Hi Ellen,

Guess what? Tim takes me to the cinema last night and today when I was studying at home he came to see me and took me some flowers! I think he must be in love with me!

Bye,

Marian

Wednesday 5 March 2010
Dear Marian,
Yes, I think Tim is in love with you! Why don't you brought him to our party on Friday so we can all meet him? Oh, and take that new CD you told me about, I'd like to hear it.
Love,
Ellen

Thursday 6 March 2010

Hi again Ellen,

Thanks for inviting Tim. He said yes.

I'll bring the CD to the party tomorrow and I'll leave it with you. You can take it back when you come to see me on Sunday.

Take care,

Marian.

Your score
/30

Get / got / got

43.1
10 marks

Fill the gaps in 1–5 with an adjective (e.g. *dark*, *hot*, etc.). Fill the gaps in 6–10 with a noun (e.g. *stamps*, *doctor*, etc.).

Example: If you are ill, you want to get ....*well/better*.... .

1 If you are cold, you want to get ....
2 If your life is boring, you want it to get more ....
3 If your working day is very long, you'd like it to get ....
4 If you are poor, you'd probably like to get ....
5 If someone is fat and they eat less and do a lot of exercise they will probably get
....

Example: If you are hungry, you want to get some ..*food*..............

6 Before you go on a train journey, you have to get a ....
7 You go to the bank or a cash machine when you want to get some ....
8 You go to the baker's when you want to get some ....
9 When it's your birthday you probably get some ....
10 You check your email program to see if you have got any new ....

43.2
10 marks

Use the words in brackets and the pictures to ask questions with *get to*.

Example: (How / I / ?)

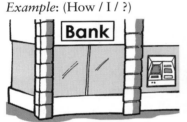

How do I get to the bank?

1 (When / you / ?)

2 (What time / you / yesterday / ?)

3 (How / I / ?)

4 (When / your brother / on Monday / ?)

5 (How / I / ?)

....

43.3
10 marks

Fill the gaps using the correct forms of *get* / phrases with *get*.

Example: Dick is planning to go to university ....*to get*.......... a degree in medicine.

1 It's raining and the people at the bus stop .... wet.
2 David and Hilary .... last week. They're on their honeymoon now.
3 I'm very thirsty. I'd like .... a cup of tea now.
4 My dad usually .... from work at 6.30.
5 My grandfather was ill last week but, happily, he .... now.
6 I'd like a change. I'd love to .... in a big international company.
7 What time do you usually .... school in the morning?
8 My brother .... from the United States yesterday.
9 I want to know what's happening in the world. I'm going to the newsagent's to
....

Your score
/30

10 I love sending and .... emails.

44.1 Fill the gaps in these magazine horoscopes.

10 marks

PISCES

Your boss will give you the chance of a much better job this week. Say yes immediately; don't (1)........................... it down. If you (2)........................... on working in your present job for another two or three years, you will have a very interesting career, but if you get impatient and (3)........................... off and look for another job, it could be a big mistake.

CAPRICORN

It's time to start a new, active life! Don't stay in bed. Start getting (4)........................... early in the mornings. (5)........................... off the bus before your stop and walk the rest of the way home. In the evenings, (6)........................... the TV off, (7)........................... your coat on and go for a walk. (8)........................... on! Start living!

GEMINI

You have too much stress in your life. You must learn to relax. Every evening, (9)........................... on the TV, lie on the sofa, (10)........................... off your shoes and forget your problems for an hour.

44.2 Match the sentences on the left with the sentences on the right.

10 marks

1 The bus came.	ᵁ a She turned it up.
2 She felt too warm in her thick jacket.	⁵ b She turned the light on.
3 The plane was delayed.	²c She took it off.
4 She couldn't hear the radio.	₁ d She got on it.
5 It was dark in the room.	₃e It took off at 4.45 pm.

44.3 Correct the mistakes.

10 marks

1 I have to get the train at 7.30 tomorrow morning, so I'll have to go up early.
2 I went over working until after midnight because I had an exam the next day.
3 It's raining; put over your raincoat.
4 They offered her the job but she turned it off.
5 If you go off the bus at Histon Street, you will see the museum on your left.

Your score
/30

Everyday things

45.1
5 marks

Andy does these things every morning. What time does he do each thing?

Andy _wakes up_ at seven o'clock. Then he ⁽¹⁾........................ at five past seven. He
⁽²⁾........................ at ten past seven and ⁽³⁾........................ at quarter past seven. At quarter to
eight he ⁽⁴⁾........................ and at half past eight he leaves the house and ⁽⁵⁾........................ .

45.2
5 marks

Andy does these things every evening. What time does he do each thing?

| finishes work   has dinner   watches TV   goes to bed   comes home   makes dinner |

Example: 5.00   _finishes work_

1 5.30 ....
2 6.30 ....

3 7.00 ....
4 8.30 ....

5 11.00 ....

45.3
10 marks

Here are pictures of Andy. What is he doing in each picture? Write sentences.

Example: _Andy is leaving the office._

45.4
10 marks

Write questions for these answers. Use either *What time ...?* or *How often ...?*

Example: Q: _How often do you listen to the radio?_
A: I listen to the radio every evening.

1 Q: ....
   A: I go to work at 8.15.
2 Q: ....
   A: I clean the house every Saturday.
3 Q: ....
   A: I usually get up at 7 o'clock.
4 Q: ....
   A: I go for a walk every evening.
5 Q: ....
   A: I wash my clothes every week.

6 Q: ....
   A: I usually go to bed at 11.30.
7 Q: ....
   A: I go to the supermarket once a week.
8 Q: ....
   A: I usually come home at 6.30.
9 Q: ....
   A: I go to my friend's house every
       Friday evening.
10 Q: ....
   A: I write a letter to my grandmother
       every Sunday.

46.1
5 marks

Match the sentence beginnings on the left with the correct endings on the right.

1 I said   **a** me her name.
2 She told   **b** happy birthday to him.
3 I told her   **c** goodbye to each other.
4 They said   **d** the way to the station.
5 We said   **e** that they were tired.

46.2
5 marks

Fill the gaps with the correct form of *say* or *tell*.

1   LARRY: Did she .... what time she was arriving?
           RUBY: Yes, her train arrives at 6.30.
2   MICK: Have you .... Jim about the party?
           FRAN: Yes, I've invited him.
3   YOLANDA: Did she .... thanks when you found her credit card?
         PAULA: No, she just took it. You know what she's like.
4   EILEEN: Did Bob .... any jokes at the dinner yesterday?
            KIM: Yes, as usual he had some very funny ones.
5   TOURIST: Can you .... me when the concert starts, please?
LOCAL PERSON: Yes, 7.30.

46.3
10 marks

What do you do in these situations? Use the verb *ask* in your answer.

Example: You are in a new city and want to know what to see, where to eat, etc.
        Ask for information (e.g. at the tourist office)

1 You do not know how to get from place A to place B.
2 You are in the street and you don't have your watch on.
3 You are in class and you do not understand a new word.
4 You have finished your meal in a restaurant.
5 Someone is playing a CD very loudly and you are trying to study.

46.4
10 marks

Correct the mistakes in these sentences.

1 The phone's ringing! Will you reply to it, please, David?
2 My best friend lived in Denmark for five, years so she talks excellent Danish.
3 I sent him an email, but he hasn't said back yet.
4 SVEN: How is said 'Milan' in Italian?
   LENA: It's 'Milano'.
5 He said me an interesting story about when he was a child.

Your score
/30

47.1 What is each person doing? Write a sentence, using one of the verbs from the box.

0 marks

| carry | climb | dance | drive | fall | fly | jump | ride | ~~run~~ | swim | walk |

Example:

He's running.

1

2

3

4

5

6

7

8

9

10

47.2 Choose the correct word to complete each sentence. Circle the correct answer.

0 marks

Example: We'll .... a bus to town.   a) arrive b) (take) c) go

1 Please could you .... me the bread.   a) carry b) pass c) take
2 Please be quick or we'll .... the train.   a) catch b) take c) miss
3 What time does the plane .... in Rome?   a) arrive b) fly c) get
4 He can .... a bus.   a) ride b) drive c) go
5 How did you .... to Paris?   a) take b) get c) arrive
6 Can you .... a horse?   a) drive b) go c) ride
7 Let's .... the underground.   a) go b) take c) fly
8 If we run, we'll .... the bus.   a) miss b) go c) catch
9 Pilots .... planes.   a) fly b) drive c) ride
10 We can .... to Munich by train.   a) take b) pass c) go

47.3 Fill the gaps with the correct form of the words in the box (e.g. *go, goes* or *going*).

0 marks

Example: I love ....*going*........... places by ship.

| carry | catch | dance | drive | fall | fly | ~~go~~ | ride | run | swim | walk |

1 At the sports club the children enjoy .... round the track, ... in the pool and .... their bikes.
2 You need a licence to .... a car or .... a plane.
3 On Friday evening we all go .... at a nightclub.
4 We must leave now if we want to .... the early train.
5 Waiters get a lot of exercise. They .... miles every day as they .... food from the kitchen to the tables.
6 I don't like heights – I'm afraid of ....

Talking about language

48.1
20 marks

Complete the table with the correct word from the box.

preposition   phrase   noun   paragraph   adjective   plural
adverb   sentence   dialogue   ~~verb~~   singular

	Grammar word	Meaning	Example
	verb	something we do	go, eat, look
1		a piece of text (one or more sentences) beginning on a new line	This test is about words for talking about language. You can score 30 points.
2		a word that describes a verb	quickly, happily
3		a conversation between two people	TOM: Where's my pen? NORA: On the table.
4		just one	car, student, girl
5		a person or thing	teacher, cat, chair
6		a word that describes a person or thing	big, good, tall
7		a complete idea in writing; it starts with a (capital letter) and ends in a (full stop) (.)	(Y)esterday I went to the beach with a friend (.)
8		a little word used before a noun	at, on, from
9		a group of words	in my room, a new car
10		more than one	cars, students, girls

48.2
10 marks

Answer the questions.

1 What is the plural of *boy*: *boys or boy's*?
2 Is *nice* an adjective or an adverb?
3 Which word is the verb in this sentence? *My sister works in Hong Kong.*
4 What is the singular of *men*?
5 Which of these words is a noun: *sing, out, long, door*?
6 Which of these words is a preposition: *the, at, because*?
7 Which of these words is an adverb: *go, front, easily, full*?
8 Which word is not a noun: *cat, student, music, put*?
9 Which of these words is plural: *egg, bicycle, children, house*?
10 A dialogue is a conversation between two people. True or false?

Your score
/30

Conjunctions and connecting words

49.1 Choose a word from the box to fill the gap in each sentence. Use each word once only.

0 marks

when   or   also   so   before   because   and   after   if   but

1 .... I went to sleep, I set my alarm clock for seven o'clock .... I had to get up early to go to the airport.
2 .... I win a lot of money one day, I'll stop working .... travel round the world.
3 You can cross the English Channel by ferry .... through the tunnel.
4 I like apples. I .... like oranges, ... I don't like bananas.
5 .... she left university she got a job in her uncle's company.
6 I'm going to study this evening, ... please don't phone me.
7 Phone me .... you get to London, so I know you are OK.

49.2 Choose the correct explanation. Circle the correct answer.

0 marks

1 BOB: I don't want to marry you because we're too young for marriage.
SALLY: Hmm.
a) Bob would like to marry Sally because she is so young.
b) Bob thinks he and Sally are too young to get married.
c) Bob thinks he is too young for Sally and he doesn't want to marry her.
2 HILDA: My hair and face are like my sister's but I'm taller than her.
EVA: Really?
a) Hilda likes her sister's hair and face but her sister is smaller.
b) Hilda's face and hair are similar to her sister's and they are both the same height.
c) Hilda's face and hair are similar to her sister's but her sister is shorter than she is.
3 GEORGE: My brother and I both play the guitar but I play the violin too.
JOE: Oh yes?
a) George plays one more instrument than his brother.
b) George plays the violin and his brother plays the violin.
c) George only plays the violin; his brother only plays the guitar.
4 JAKE: When I go to university I'll study maths.
RITA: Mm. Good.
a) Jake thinks it's possible he will go to university and study maths.
b) Jake prefers to study maths; he doesn't want to go to university.
c) Jake has decided he will go to university and study maths.
5 DENISE: Luke played the piano. He sang as well.
GUDRUN: Did he?
a) Luke played the piano and sang very well.
b) Luke played the piano and sang.
c) Luke played the piano but didn't sing.

49.3 Find five sentences that make sense in this table.

10 marks

	and	I've finished secondary school.
	so	I want to learn more about other countries and cultures.
I'm going to study abroad	when	I'm really looking forward to it.
	if	I will be away from home for three years.
	because	I get good grades in my exams.

Test 50 Days, months, seasons

50.1
10 marks

Which month is this?

Example: the 3rd month <u>March</u>

1	the 6th month	....
2	the 12th month	....
3	the 8th month	....
4	the 1st month	....
5	the 7th month	....
6	the 10th month	....
7	the 2nd month	....
8	the 9th month	....
9	the 4th month	....
10	the 11th month	....

50.2
10 marks

Match the words on the left with the definitions on the right.

1	afternoon	a	the day before today
2	century	b	Saturday and Sunday
3	day	c	the coldest season
4	evening	d	60 seconds
5	fortnight	e	7 days
6	minute	f	between 12 pm and 6 pm
7	tomorrow	g	24 hours
8	week	h	after 6 pm
9	weekend	i	the day after today
10	winter	j	14 days
11	yesterday	k	100 years

50.3
10 marks

Fill the gap with the correct preposition.

Example: I had lunch with my aunt ....on.......... Saturday.

1 Today is Monday. So the day .... tomorrow is Wednesday.
2 We had a lovely holiday .... the summer last year. We went to France .... July.
3 I am going to stay with Sophie .... the weekend. We're going to the cinema .... Friday evening and then we're going to see my grandma .... Saturday.
4 There are seven days .... a week and 366 days .... a leap year.
5 We had an important meeting the day .... yesterday.
6 My brother's birthday is .... the spring.

Your score
/30

Time words

51.1 Fill the gaps.
5 marks

1 It's four .... in the afternoon now.
2 Oscar came home at 2 pm. He came home two
....
3 Oscar has been home .... two ....

51.2 Answer the questions.
5 marks

It's April now.

1 Which month is next month?
2 Which month was last month?
3 Which month was it two months ago?
4 How long is Bill on holiday for?
5 It's Saturday 16 April today. What date will it
be next Saturday?

51.3 How often? Put the words on the steps, from *not at all* to *every time*.
0 marks

sometimes   often   usually
always   very rarely   never
rarely   now and then
occasionally   not often

every time

not at all

51.4 Put the words on the right in the correct places in these sentences.
5 marks

1 Millie is afraid of flying so she........................ travels on a plane.
She .... goes by train.   ALWAYS / NEVER
2 I meet him .... at the sports club, but I don't see
him ....   OFTEN / NOW AND THEN
3 It .... snows in the south of the country. It ....
rains instead, because it's warmer than the north.   USUALLY / RARELY
4 NINA: How often do you buy new clothes?
RACHEL: Well, ... I'm a student, so I only have
enough money to buy clothes ....   NOT OFTEN / OCCASIONALLY
5 .... I love studying, but .... I start to feel
tired if I read for a long time.   SOMETIMES / USUALLY

51.5 Complete the second sentence so that it means the same as the first one in each case.
5 marks

1 Right now, Ken takes the bus in the morning and again in the evening.
.... the ...., Ken takes the bus .... a day.
2 I'll be back after a minute or so. See you in a very short time!
I'll be back .... moment. See you .... !
3 Bill phones his sister every Friday. She was ill a short time ago.
Bill phones his sister .... a week. She was ill ....
4 Many years ago, people used horses, not cars.
In .... , people used horses, not cars.
5 Many years from now, people will travel to the moon for their holidays.
In .... , people will travel to the moon for their holidays.

our score
/30

52.1
10 marks
Match these words with their opposites.

Example: at home – out

~~at home~~ back beginning bottom end front here left ~~out~~ right there top

52.2
10 marks
Look at the pictures and answer the questions.

Example: | A E I O U | Which letter is in the middle? ....I..........

1 What is there on the front of the car?

2 What is there on the back of the car?

3 What is there on the side of the car?

8 Where is the photograph? .... Lucy's desk.

4 What is at the beginning of the path?

5 Who is in the middle of the path?

6 What is at the end of the path?

9 Where is the boy sitting? .... the front of the class.

7 Where is Joe? .... the kitchen.

10 Where is Tokyo? .... Japan.

Tokyo

52.3
10 marks
Choose the best words from the box to fill the gaps in the email.

abroad ~~at home~~ away back everywhere here left middle out side there

New Message

File Edit View Insert Format Tools Message Help

Hi Mia,

I'm writing this from my computer at home........... . No one else is (1)............................. . The children are (2)............................. at a friend's house just down the street, and Will is (3)............................. for a few days. He's on business (4)............................. , in a small town in the (5)............................. of France. He'll be (6)............................. on Friday.

He's just sent me an email to say that it's lovely and hot (7).............................! I can only see rain from the window on my (8)............................. as I type, and the TV says that it's raining (9)............................. in this country.

I wanted to plant some flowers at the (10)............................. of our house but it's too wet to be in the garden.

So I'm just going to read a book until it's time for the children to come home.

Love,

Tina

Your score /30

start Outlook Express New Message EN

Manner

53.1
0 marks

Put pairs of opposite words into the table.

Opposites	
right	wrong

good	fast
quiet	sad
friendly	~~right~~
slow	bad
loud	unfriendly
~~wrong~~	happy

53.2
0 marks

Fill the gaps with an adverb (e.g. *wrongly*) so that the second sentence means the same as the first.

Example: The numbers in this list are wrong.

This list is ....*wrongly*........ numbered.

1 He was driving at 140 kilometres per hour.
He was driving very ....
2 He shouted her name.
He said her name very ....
3 We went past the baby's bedroom, making very little noise because she was asleep.
We went past the room very ....
4 He's a good pianist.
He plays the piano really ....
5 There was ice on the road, so we drove at 20 kilometres per hour.
We drove very ....
6 She was very unfriendly when she spoke to us.
She spoke to us .... very unfriendly ....
7 I don't swim for the school team because I'm a bad swimmer.
I swim very ....
8 The manager was quick to reply to my letter.
The manger replied to my letter ....
9 She looked at me in a very sad way.
She looked at me very ....
10 Our teacher is always friendly when she corrects our mistakes.
She always corrects our mistakes ....

53.3
0 marks

Answer the questions, using adverb forms of the words in the box. Write full sentences.

sudden   quiet   strange   quick   easy

1 I can't hear what the child is saying.
How is the child speaking?
2 Glen was acting in a way that no one could understand.
How was Glen acting?
3 The accident happened in one short moment, and no one was expecting it.
How did the accident happen?
4 Pippa passed the exam with no problems at all.
How did she pass the exam?
5 He finished the job in less than a minute.
How did he finish the job?

Your score
/30

Common uncountable nouns

54.1
10 marks

Write the uncountable noun for each picture. We give you the first letter each time.

1 i..............................

2 a..............................

3 w..............................

4 f..............................

5 l..............................

54.2
10 marks

Put these nouns into two columns: countable and uncountable.

| ~~banana~~ milk shoe money rice bread traffic apple bus plate butter |

Countable	Uncountable
banana	

54.3
10 marks

Correct the mistakes.

1 Are these furnitures new? I haven't seen them before. (2 marks)
2 We had a terrible weather last week!
3 We have ten people coming to lunch, so we'll need three large breads.
4 Can you give me some advices about English courses in the UK?
5 The traffics are always very bad around 8 o'clock in the morning.
6 The news are on TV in five minutes. Shall we watch them? (2 marks)
7 Rail travels are more interesting than going by air.
8 I have a lot of works to do before the exam next week.

Your score
/30

55 Common adjectives 1: Good and bad things

55.1 Put these adjectives into the correct columns.
0 marks

> ~~awful~~ dreadful excellent great horrible lovely
> marvellous nice perfect terrible wonderful

Good	Bad
	awful

55.2 Circle the correct underlined adjective in these sentences.
0 marks

Example: Harry is a nice/(dreadful) man – nobody likes him.

1 I love Kay's new car – it's <u>great/awful</u>.
2 I don't like my boss – he's <u>wonderful/horrible</u>.
3 Let's go to Max's Restaurant tonight – the food there is <u>nasty/excellent</u>.
4 Pete didn't enjoy the film – he said it was <u>awful/brilliant</u>.
5 Sue did very well in her test – the teacher said she wrote a <u>terrible/brilliant</u> essay.
6 The party was <u>terrible/lovely</u> – everyone had a good time.
7 Thank you so much – I had a <u>perfect/horrible</u> day.
8 Jo does very well at school – she usually gets <u>good/bad</u> marks in her class.
9 We're planning to have a picnic tomorrow – I hope the weather is <u>fine/terrible</u>.
10 The hotel was <u>awful/marvellous</u> – we'll never go there again.

55.3 Fill the gaps in these dialogues. We give you the first letter each time.
0 marks

Example: A: I had a great time at the party last night.
　　　　 B: Good.................... !

1 A: Let's meet at 7 – OK?
　 B: P.............................
2 A: What dreadful weather!
　 B: Yes, isn't it t............................. ?
3 A: I'll send you a postcard from our holiday.
　 B: L............................. !
4 A: The film was terrible, wasn't it!
　 B: Yes, it was h............................. !
5 A: The food is good here, isn't it?
　 B: Yes, it's m............................. !
6 A: I'll show you the town tomorrow.
　 B: E............................. !
7 A: I don't like her very much, do you?
　 B: No, she's a............................. !
8 A: I'll help you paint your room if you like.
　 B: W............................. !
9 A: It's a beautiful view, isn't it?
　 B: Yes, it's g............................. !
10 A: Did you enjoy the party?
　 B: No, it was d............................. !

56.1 Put these adjectives into the correct columns.
10 marks

> ~~nice~~ kind horrible unhappy wonderful stupid
> difficult easy-going lovely selfish naughty

Positive	Negative
nice	

56.2 Circle the correct underlined adjectives in this email.
10 marks

Delete   Reply   Reply All   Forward   Print

Hi Jenna,
Before you come with us on our club picnic, let me tell you about some of the people in the group.
Harry, our club president, is a (nice)/ horrible man – everybody likes him. And I like Karen too – she's
(1) lovely/selfish. I don't like Brenda – she's (2) wonderful/horrible, but other people think she's okay. I
don't want to sit near Robert – he's a (3) difficult/wonderful person. Henry is always very (4) selfish/kind to
me, so we can sit with him, and we all like Jeremy. We think he's a (5) wonderful/horrible person.
Krishnan is always laughing. He's such a (6) happy/difficult person. Jo is home from university – she's
(7) naughty/intelligent, just like her older sister. The only problem is, she's bringing her little brother Jack
and her little sister Emma with her. Jack is very (8) wonderful/naughty at school. The teacher often has to
send him to the head teacher's office, Jo tells me. The good news is that Emma is a (9) well-behaved/
difficult child, and all her teachers like her.
By the way, it was very (10) kind/stupid of me to forget your mother's birthday. I hope she wasn't upset?
See you Saturday!
Love,
Barbara

56.3 Find the opposites of the words in Box A in Box B.
10 marks

A

kind	happy	lovely
stupid	easy-going	

B

intelligent	difficult	
unhappy	selfish	horrible

Your score
/30

Words and prepositions

57.1 *Match the sentence beginnings on the left with the endings on the right.*

0 marks

1 Wait at this stop   a for the lovely flowers.
2 Nurses look   b for our train tickets.
3 I'm looking forward   c at playing the violin.
4 She thanked him   d to my brother.
5 I'm not very interested e for arriving late.
6 I'll pay   f for the number 10 bus.
7 The child is afraid   g in politics.
8 I must apologise   h for four cups of coffee.
9 Suzie is very good   i after people in hospital.
10 This coat belongs   j of big dogs.
11 James asked the waiter k to the holidays.

57.2 *Fill the gaps in each sentence with the correct preposition.*

0 marks

Example: I won't be long. Please wait ....**for**.......... me.

1 I can't find my glasses. Can you help me look .... them?
2 Who does that car belong .... ?
3 Jane was very proud .... her son when he won first prize.
4 We're thinking .... going to Spain for our holiday.
5 Sally is bad .... maths but she is very good .... English.
6 I'm looking forward .... seeing you soon.
7 Dick apologised .... breaking the window.
8 Please look .... the statue on the right.
9 I'm not interested .... old buildings.

57.3 *Fill the gaps in this email with the correct verbs or adjectives.*

0 marks

New Message
File Edit View Insert Format Tools Message Help

Thanks for your email. I (1) .... for not replying sooner, but I've been very busy. I had a maths exam today. I'm not very (2) .... at maths, so I had to do a lot of work for it. I have to (3) .... for my results – I won't get them for a week or two.

Now I'm free!!! This evening I'm going to (4) .... to a new CD which Mum bought me today. We went to the shops together after my exam and I was going to (5) .... for it but Mum said she'd buy it for me. She said she was (6) .... of me because I'd worked so hard for my exam. I hope she feels the same when I get the results!

How are things with you? Will you be able to (7) .... to my party next month? I hope so! I liked the photo you sent me. Does the skateboard you're standing on (8) .... to you? Aren't you (9) .... of falling off?

I (10) .... forward to your next message.

Bye for now,

Natasha

start   Outlook Express   New Message   EN

58.1 Read the instructions. Use a prefix with the word on the left to complete the table.

10 marks

Word	Instruction	Answer
possible	Make an adjective with the opposite meaning.	impossible
1 war	Make an adjective meaning 'before the war'.	
2 smoking	Make an adjective which means 'you must not smoke here'.	
3 price	Make an adjective that means '50% of the price'.	
4 send	Make a verb that means 'send something again'.	
5 girlfriend	Make a noun that means 'someone who was someone's girlfriend but is not any more'.	
6 happy	Make an adjective with the opposite meaning.	
7 comfortable	Make an adjective with the opposite meaning.	
8 tell	Make a verb that means 'tell something again'.	
9 formal	Make an adjective with the opposite meaning.	
10 finished	Make an adjective with the opposite meaning.	

58.2 Rewrite the sentences, using a word with the prefix given. Do not change the meaning.

10 marks

Example: Mr Trottman is not popular with the students. (*un*)

<u>Mr Trottman is unpopular with the students.</u>

1 He was the president of the club but he isn't any more. (*ex*)
2 I prefer drinks that have no alcohol. (*non*)
3 I think you should write your essay again. (*re*)
4 He does not seem to be happy in his job. (*un*)
5 The restaurant has meals for children which cost only half the normal price. (*half*)
6 I don't like to give homework that I haven't finished to my teacher. (*un*)
7 The years before they start school are very important for little children. (*pre*)
8 It is not possible for anyone to live for 200 years. (*im*)
9 You can wear clothes that are not formal to the party. (*in*)
10 This chair is not comfortable. (*un*)

58.3 Correct the mistakes.

10 marks

1 This machine is insafe. Don't use it.
2 Every sentence in this section has something non-correct in it.
3 It is inpossible at the moment for human beings to travel to other galaxies.
4 Do you ever get ex-exam nerves?
5 I still have some inread books from the library. I must read them.
6 The lessons are very unformal and we like the teacher very much.
7 Mike isn't my boss any more. I have a new one. Mike is my pre-boss.
8 Years ago, you always had to say if you wanted a smoking or unsmoking seat on a plane.
9 It is only a halfhour drive from here to the airport.
10 I unaddressed the letter because it was for a person who had moved to a new address.

Your score
/30

59.1 Look at the suffixes in the table. What do they mean? Add another example for
each suffix.

	Suffix	Meaning of suffix	Example
hope*ful*, use*ful*, beauti*ful*	ful	full of	painful
1 work*er*, writ*er*, instruct*or*	er, or		
2 cook*er*, calculat*or*, hairdry*er*	er, or		
3 use*less*, sleep*less*, pain*less*	less		
4 happi*ness*, sad*ness*, kind*ness*	ness		
5 sand*y*, sunn*y*, rain*y*	y		

59.2 What are these things or people?

Example: a thing for opening tins.

<u>a tin opener</u>

1 a thing for drying your hair
2 a person who swims
3 a thing for opening bottles
4 a person who builds something
5 a person who travels
6 a person who writes
7 a thing that cooks food
8 a person who teaches
9 a thing that sharpens pencils
10 a person who sings

59.3 Put the letters in the right order to make a word and then match each phrase to the
correct picture.

Example: I've got a new T R A L L U C O C A. <u>calculator – a</u>

1 He's smiling L A P Y P H I.
2 It's a N U N Y S day.
3 It's a D A Y N S beach.
4 It's an electric R O C K O E.
5 It's a A I N Y R day.

a

b

c

d

e

f

Words you may confuse

60.1
10 marks

Circle the correct answer.

1 The opposite of *loud* is …
   a) quite.   b) quiet.

2 The past tense of *fall* is …
   a) felt.   b) fell.

3 The opposite of *tight* is …
   a) loose.   b) lose.

4 A *cooker* is …
   a) a person.   b) a thing.

5 The opposite of *find* is …
   a) loose.   b) lose.

6 The past tense of *feel* is …
   a) felt.   b) fell.

7 A police officer .... your driving licence.
   a) checks   b) controls

8 *Very* and .... can both be used before *big*, *small*, *nice*, etc.
   a) quiet   b) quite

9 If you need something, you can often .... it from a friend.
   a) lend   b) borrow

10 People stand at a bus stop to .... a bus.
   a) expect   b) wait for

60.2
10 marks

Choose a word from the box which ends in the same sound as the word in the table.

shoes belt fight diet juice ~~bell~~

Word	Same sound
fell	bell
1 quiet	
2 lose	
3 quite	
4 felt	
5 loose	

60.3
10 marks

Correct the mistakes in these sentences.

1 I borrowed her my pen and she never gave it back to me.
2 My brother is a really good cooker. I love eating at his house.
3 Yesterday I felt down the stairs and hurt my leg.
4 I haven't done enough work, so I'm waiting to fail my exam.
5 Can I lend your tennis racket? I'll bring it back tomorrow.
6 They control your age before you can get into the nightclub. You must be 18.
7 I arrived at Rod and Fiona's house at 3.30 pm and said 'Good evening' to everyone.
8 The exam tomorrow is very important, so I expect I pass it with a good grade.
9 I was surprised that nobody controlled my ID in the bank. They just gave me the money!
10 Her new flat is quiet big, so she can invite friends to stay.

Your score
/30

Answer key

Notes on the Answer key and marking scheme

1 Each test has a total of 30 marks.
2 There is one mark for each correct answer in most exercises. Sometimes there is half $\frac{1}{2}$ a mark or two marks for each correct answer. You will find the total marks for each exercise below the exercise number on the test page, and on the right-hand side in the answer key.
3 If two answers are given in the key (separated by a slash /), both answers are correct (e.g. 'They're having lunch/dinner').
4 Where the answer to one of the questions is given in the text as an example, it appears in brackets […] in the answer key.

Test 1

1.1
1 daughter
2 uncle
3 son
4 sister/brother
5 father
6 grandmother
7 grandson
8 grandfather
9 aunt
10 grandparents / grandmother and grandfather (10 marks)

1.2

Across	Down
1 daughter	2 uncle
4 cousin	3 nephew
7 parents	5 sister
8 come	6 nieces
10 any	9 only

(10 marks)

1.3
1 NO (My *uncle* John is my mother's sister's husband. / My nephew John is *my sister's/brother's son*.)
2 YES
3 NO (Mary is David's *wife*. / David is Mary's husband.)
4 YES
5 NO (two *wives* and two *children*)

(10 marks)

Test 2

2.1
1 were   3 honeymoon   5 died   7 call; after
2 got; to   4 married   6 of   8 ill   (10 marks)

2.2 1 widowed   2 married   3 divorced   4 single   (4 marks)

2.3
1 They are getting married.
2 A wedding
3 The honeymoon   (6 marks: 2 each)

2.4
1 How much does/did he weigh?; What are they going to call him? / What are they calling him?
2 What did he die of?; When is the funeral?
3 Where did they go on/for (their) honeymoon?

(10 marks: 2 each)

Test 3

3.1

1 shoulder	5 knee	9 heart
2 stomach	6 nose	10 leg
3 finger	7 mouth	
4 thumb	8 neck	

```
A T M T O O T H
S H O U L D E R
T U U N E C K F
O M T N M O M I
M B H O P A R N
A G E S A L E G
C A R E K N E E
H E A R T I P R
```

(10 marks: ½ for labelling each picture and ½ for each word found)

3.2

1 eyes; ears	5 blood	8 thumb
2 hair; nails	6 brain	9 back/side/front
3 chest; neck	7 skin	10 like 'ch' in *chemist*
4 waist; hips		

(14 marks)

3.3

1 Her *hair is* black.	4 Please wash *your* hands
2 a pain in *his* side	5 My *feet* hurt. (or My *foot hurts.*)
3 two *teeth*	6 put *their* hands up

(6 marks)

Test 4

4.1

1 socks	3 shirt	5 boots	7 coat	9 hat	11 T-shirt
2 belt	4 tie	6 skirt	8 scarf	10 gloves	12 trainers

(12 marks)

4.2 1 why 2 run 3 note 4 suit 5 half (5 marks)

4.3 trousers tights jeans shorts sunglasses (5 marks)

4.4

1 when you get up	5 jumper
2 a ring	6 Robert is carrying an umbrella.
3 a woman	7 Lisa has put a skirt on.
4 a suit	8 At night, I *get undressed* and go to bed.

(8 marks)

Test 5

5.1

Eyes	Skin	Hair	Height and weight
dark	dark	dark	fat
green	fair	fair	short
brown	brown	brown	slim
		short	tall
		long	thin*

* We can also talk about 'thin hair' if someone does not have very much hair.

(10 marks: ½ if you do not put the word in all the possible columns)

5.2 1 No, she's got *short, dark* hair. (2 marks)
2 No, she's *tall* and *thin/slim*. (2 marks)
3 No, he's/she's *old/elderly*.
4 No, he's *good-looking*.
5 No, she's got *dark/black/brown* hair.
6 No, he's *fat/overweight*.
7 No, she's *average-looking/ugly*.
8 No, he/she's *short*.   (10 marks)

5.3 1 He's got a beard/moustache.
2 He's also got a moustache/beard.
3 His skin is dark/brown.
4 He's got short/dark/brown/black hair.
5 He is good-looking/young.   (5 marks)

(Note: other answers are possible. Give yourself a mark for each correct answer.)

5.4 1 How tall are you?
2 How heavy is the baby?
3 How much does the child weigh?
4 What does your new teacher look like?
5 What colour is her hair?   (5 marks)

Test 6

6.1 1 d   2 e   3 a   4 b   5 c   (10 marks)

6.2 1 headache   2 malaria   3 asthma   4 cancer   5 cholera   (5 marks)

6.3 1 cholera   2 asthma   3 cancer   4 headache   5 malaria   (5 marks)

6.4 1 stressed; relax   5 Exercise
2 attack; hospital   6 cold
3 hay fever; sneeze   7 aspirin
4 diet   (10 marks)

Test 7

7.1 1 You feel hungry.   5 You feel ill.   9 You feel sad.
2 You feel tired.   6 You feel cold.   10 You feel surprised.
3 You feel angry.   7 You feel happy.
4 You feel thirsty.   8 You feel hot.   (10 marks)

7.2 1 hate   2 hot   3 sad/unhappy   4 well   (4 marks)

7.3 1 I like tennis very much. Or: I very much like tennis.
2 I am very happy *about* your good exam results.
3 Jack hopes his girlfriend will phone him soon. Or: Jack wants his girlfriend to phone him soon.
4 I really like ice cream.
5 My little sister prefers juice *to* milk.
6 Grandfather is *a* little tired today.   (6 marks)

7.4 1 Bonnie looks *upset*.   6 Rob looks *cold*.
2 Colin looks *angry*.   7 Nat looks *tired*.
3 Stan looks *sad*.   8 Clare looks *happy*.
4 Katie looks *ill*.   9 Spot looks *thirsty*.
5 Mark looks surprised.   10 Fluffy looks hungry.   (10 marks)

Test 8

8.1 1 Good *morning*.
2 Good *evening*. (Note: Not 'Goodnight'. You say 'Goodnight' when you leave, not when you arrive.)
3 *Cheers*, everybody!
4 *Excuse me*, please.
5 *Bless you*!   (10 marks)

8.2 1 Hello/Hi   6 Happy birthday!
2 Hi/Hello   7 Congratulations!
3 How are you?   8 good luck!
4 And you?   9 see you soon.
5 Not too bad, thanks.   10 Goodbye.   (10 marks)

8.3 1 LIM: Chinese New Year starts this week.
       DEREK: Oh really? *Happy* New Year!
    2 DIANE: Here's the newspaper you asked me to get.
       NORBERT: *Thanks / Thank you.*
       DIANE: No problem.
    3 RUTH: This is my last day in the office till December 28th.
       WILL: Oh, well, I'll say *Happy/Merry* Christmas, then.
       RUTH: Thanks. You too.
    4 GEOFF: I swam a kilometre today.
       FRAN: Well *done*! You must be very fit.
       GEOFF: Yeah, I feel good.
    5 BETH: It's my birthday today.
       SONYA: Oh, *happy birthday*!
       BETH: Thank you.   (10 marks)

Test 9

9.1 1 Why
2 really
3 mind
4 up
5 What
6 Let's
7 around
8 anyway
9 dear
10 Absolutely   (10 marks)

9.2 1 Well done!
2 Hurry up!
3 Look out!
4 What a pity!
5 It doesn't matter!   (10 marks: 1 for completing the expression
                                                and 1 for matching it to the right situation)

9.3
1 else
2 matter
3 actually
4 don't
5 going
6 around
7 meet
8 really
9 out
10 Anyway (10 marks)

Test 10

10.1
1 **Down** **Across**
  1 onion   3 oranges
  2 grapes   4 banana
      5 pear
2 **Across** **Down**
  1 pineapple   5 potatoes
  2 carrots
  3 tomatoes
  4 beans (10 marks)

10.2
1 Pineapples   3 tomatoes   5 potatoes   7 beans   9 carrots
2 Onions   4 banana   6 Pears   8 Oranges   10 grapes   (10 marks)

10.3
1 fish 4 Strawberries
2 wine; fruit juice 5 garlic
3 pizza; hamburgers; hot-dogs 6 pasta; peas (10 marks)

Test 11

11.1
1 saucepan   3 sink   5 cooker   7 cup   9 shelf
2 cupboard   4 knife   6 microwave   8 teapot   10 frying pan
  (10 marks)

11.2
2 cloth   4 plate   6 tap   8 cooker   10 shelf
3 bowl   5 spoon   7 fridge   9 fork
The word in the grey section is *chopsticks*. (10 marks)

11.3
1 help   2 find   3 go   4 dry   5 have (5 marks)

11.4
coffee maker   washing-up liquid
kitchen roll   worktop
tea towel (5 marks)

Test 12

12.1
1 alarm clock 5 bed 9 comb
2 hairbrush 6 bedside lamp 10 bedside table
3 pyjamas 7 wardrobe
4 chest of drawers 8 dressing table (10 marks)

12.2
1 shower 6 bath
2 razor 7 shampoo
3 soap 8 toilet
4 toothpaste 9 towel
5 shelf 10 basin (10 marks)

12.3 Every morning, when my alarm clock *rings* (we often say *goes off* too) I *wake* up. Then I *get* up and *have* a shower and *get* dressed. I go downstairs and have breakfast. Then I go back to the bathroom and *clean/brush* my teeth. At the end of the day, at about 11.30, I go upstairs, *get* undressed and go *to* bed. I listen to the radio for a while, then I turn *off* the light (or *turn the light off*) and *fall* asleep.

(10 marks)

Test 13

13.1
1 armchair; sofa
2 carpet
3 bookshelf
4 TV
5 curtains
6 light
7 remote control
8 light switch
9 coffee table

(10 marks)

13.2

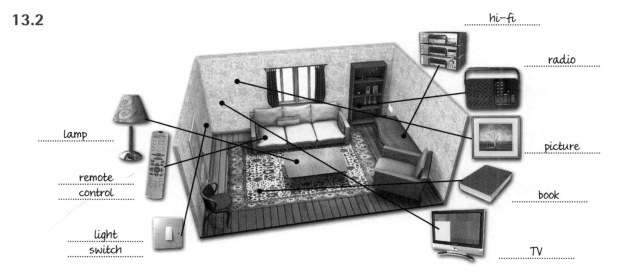

(16 marks: 1 for correct name and 1 for correct line)

13.3 1 close/shut 2 turn/switch; off 3 watch 4 relax (4 marks)

Test 14

14.1
1 a hairdresser
2 a secretary (could also be an *administrative assistant* or [informal] *an admin assistant* – see also 14.2 no. 5 below)
3 a farmer
4 a doctor
5 an engineer
6 a mechanic
7 a waiter (male or female) / waitress (female)
8 a nurse
9 a teacher
10 a shop assistant

(10 marks)

14.2
1 mechanic
2 farmer
3 hairdresser
4 teacher
5 secretary (or *personal assistant* or [informal] *PA* or *administrative assistant)*
6 shop assistant
7 engineer
8 doctor
9 nurses
10 waiters (male or female) / waitresses (female)   (10 marks)

14.3
1 False: a bus driver drives a bus.
2 True
3 False: a librarian works in a library. A person who works in a bookshop is a shop assistant or (the person who owns it) a bookseller.
4 False: a traffic warden checks parked cars.
5 True
6 False: you can say *I have interesting work* or *I have an interesting job.*
7 True
8 False: you would say *I'm a teacher.*
9 False: a person who repairs cars is called a *mechanic.*
10 True   (10 marks)

Test 15

15.1
1 geography
2 art
3 biology
4 physical education / PE
5 maths, mathematics
6 history
7 information (communication) technology / ICT / IT
8 physics
9 music
10 chemistry   (10 marks)

15.2
1 OHP – b
2 board – j or f
3 ruler – d
4 notebook – g
5 pencil – c
6 rubber – i
7 cassette – k
8 drawing pin – e
9 noticeboard – f
10 pencil sharpener – h   (10 marks)

15.3

1 doing	3 write	5 doing	7 pass; fail
2 reading	4 learn	6 ends/finishes; take/do	8 teaches

(10 marks)

Test 16

16.1

1 keyboard	3 mobile phone	5 telephone
2 letter	4 letter box	6 screen

(6 marks)

16.2   1 address   2 message   3 online   4 mouse   5 CD/disk   (10 marks: 2 each)

16.3 1 Hello.
2 Hi, can I speak to Ken?
3 He's not here right now. Who's calling?
4 It's Joanna. Could you give him a message?
5 Yeah.
6 Could you tell him I called and I'll call back later.
7 Okay, I'll tell him.
8 Thanks.
9 No problem. Bye.
10 Bye.   (10 marks)

16.4 1 Where are our holiday photos?
2 What is your email address?
3 Can I make a (phone) call?
4 What is the date on the letter? / What date is on the letter? /
On what date was the letter written?   (4 marks)

Test 17

17.1 1 traveller's cheques   6 your luggage
2 a ticket   7 a phrasebook
3 currency   8 postcards / emails / text messages
4 a package holiday   9 a rucksack (or backpack)
5 nightlife   10 a ferry   (10 marks)

17.2 1 a large comfortable *bus*   4 across *the sea*
2 they look at your *passport*   5 in a *suitcase*
3 a special *visa*   (5 marks)

17.3 1 had   6 food   11 go
2 flew   7 nightlife   12 flight
3 ferry   8 speak   13 car
4 by   9 phrasebook   14 traveller's cheques
5 by   10 going   15 currency   (15 marks)

Test 18

18.1 1 a butcher / a butcher's   5 a chemist / a chemist's / a pharmacy
2 a baker / a baker's   6 a newsagent / a newsagent's
3 a gift shop   7 a post office
4 a supermarket   8 a book shop   (8 marks)

18.2 1 electrical products / electricals
2 furniture
3 cosmetics / beauty
4 toys
5 childrenswear / children's clothes / children's clothing / kids' clothes
6 ladieswear/womenswear or ladies'/women's clothes/clothing
7 sports (equipment)
8 menswear / men's clothes / men's clothing   (8 marks)

18.3 1 CUSTOMER: The *shop assistant* said I could change it if I kept the *receipt*.
2 CUSTOMER: Where can I pay for this, please?
SHOP ASSISTANT: You can pay at that *cash desk / cash register* over there.
(*till* or *counter* is also possible)
3 SHOP ASSISTANT: Can I *help* you, madam?
CUSTOMER: Yes, how much does this hat *cost*?
SHOP ASSISTANT: Oh, let's see. Here we are – €35.

4 (In a small café)

CUSTOMER: Can I pay by *credit* card?

WAITER: Sorry, sir, we don't have a machine.

CUSTOMER: Oh. Can I write a *cheque*?

WAITER: No, I'm sorry, sir, *cash* only. This is just a small café.

5 SALLY: I like this sweater. Shall I buy it?

MARY: Why don't you *try* it on first and see how it looks on you?

SALLY: Yes, maybe I should.

6 (The customer has just bought a scarf)

SHOP ASSISTANT: There you are, madam. $25, and here's your *change*, $5. Shall I put it in a (*carrier*) *bag* for you?

CUSTOMER: No, thanks. I'll put it on. It's cold today!

7 CUSTOMER: I bought this jacket yesterday. It's too big for me. Do you have it in a smaller *size*? (12 marks)

18.4 1 b   2 a (2 marks)

Test 19

19.1
1 key	3 (tele)phone	5 lift	7 bill	9 hairdryer
2 shower	4 luggage	6 form	8 reception	10 mini-bar

(10 marks)

19.2
1 have	3 sign	5 have	7 order	9 change
2 fill in	4 Check	6 get	8 book	10 check out

(10 marks)

19.3
1 your bill
2 the lift
3 a key
4 a single room
5 a double room
6 the (country) code (for Britain)
7 a wake-up call
8 reservation/booking
9 reception
10 room service

(10 marks)

Test 20

20.1 1 d   2 e   3 f   4 b   5 a   6 c (6 marks)

20.2
1 snack
2 rare; medium; well-done
3 soft
4 list
5 starters; desserts; vegetarian
6 order

(20 marks: 2 each)

20.3
1 new potatoes
2 salmon fillet
3 fruit salad
4 apple pie

(Note: *green salad* and *fruit pie* are also possible.) (4 marks)

Test 21

21.1
1 Do you go running?
2 Do you go skiing?
3 Do you play baseball?
4 Do you play table tennis?
5 Do you go kayaking?
6 Do you go motor racing?
7 Do you go snowboarding?
8 Do you play rugby?
9 Do you play basketball?
10 Do you go swimming?

(10 marks: ½ for the sport and ½ for the right verb – *go* or *play*)

21.2
1 a swimming pool
2 a football pitch
3 a basketball court
4 skiing/snowboarding
5 a sports centre
6 judo, karate (2 marks)
7 horse racing
8 tennis / table tennis / badminton
9 motor racing

(10 marks)

21.3 1 Skiing – because all the others are done on/in water.
2 Running – because all the others use other things to help the person go faster (they use a boat or a horse or a car). / Sailing – it is done on water and all the others are done on land.
3 Badminton – because all the others use balls. / Baseball – because all the others use nets. / Volleyball – because all the others need a racquet/bat.
4 Rugby – because all the others use round balls. / Table tennis – because all the others are team sports.
5 American football – because all the others are played on a court. / Tennis – because all the others are team sports.

(10 marks: 1 for the correct sport, 1 for a correct reason)

Test 22

22.1
1 science fiction   6 comedy
2 cartoon   7 western
3 thriller   8 action
4 horror   9 romantic comedy or love story (2 marks)
5 musical

(10 marks)

22.2
1 What's on *at* the cinema
2 relax and *watch* DVDs
3 I was *bored*. / It was *boring*. ('I was boring' means <u>you</u> made other people bored!)
4 to *the* cinema
5 I enjoyed *it* very much
6 film *on* TV

(12 marks: 2 each)

22.3
1 action
2 cartoon
3 science fiction
4 comedy
5 romantic comedy/love story
6 horror
7 western (sometimes also called *cowboy films*)
8 thriller (sometimes also called *detective films*)

(8 marks)

Test 23

23.1
1 True
2 False: She is playing a computer game.
3 False: He is watching a film/western on TV.
4 False: She is gardening.
5 True
6 False: He is listening to his MP3 player.

(10 marks: 1 for correctly labelling each sentence true or false; 1 for correcting each of the four false statements)

23.2
1 having   3 phone 5 grown   7 watch   9 stay
2 had   4 cook   6 use   8 talk   10 download

(10 marks)

23.3
1 Grandfather always has a sleep after lunch. / After lunch Grandfather always has a sleep.
2 I like reading books about famous people.
3 I usually listen to the radio in my car.
4 My favourite films are musicals.
5 My mother has a lot of novels.

(10 marks)

Test 24

24.1
1	drums	5	trumpet
2	flute	6	clarinet
3	violin	7	piano
4	cello	8	guitar

(8 marks)

24.2
1 a violinist
2 a flute-player
3 a pianist
4 a trumpet-player

(8 marks: two each)

24.3
1	folk	6	can't
2	classical	7	musician
3	musical	8	has
4	music	9	download
5	band	10	to

(10 marks)

24.4
1 jazz
2 opera
3 orchestra
4 rock

(4 marks)

Test 25

25.1
Brazil and Colombia are in South America.
The USA is in North America.
Egypt and South Africa are in Africa.
India and Pakistan are in Asia.
Spain and Italy are in Europe.
New Zealand is in Australasia.

(10 marks)

25.2

Country	Adjective	Language
Argentina	Argentinian	Spanish
Canada	Canadian	French and English
China	Chinese	Chinese
Germany	German	German
Japan	Japanese	Japanese
Morocco	Moroccan	Arabic
Peru	Peruvian	Spanish
Portugal	Portuguese	Portuguese
Poland	Polish	Polish
Thailand	Thai	Thai
Tunisia	Tunisian	Arabic

(10 marks: ½ each)

25.3
1 False: Ottawa is the capital of Canada.
2 False: Dublin is the capital of Ireland.
3 True.
4 False: London is the capital of the UK.
5 False: Madrid is the capital of Spain.
6 False: Pretoria is the capital of South Africa.
7 False: Canberra is the capital of Australia.
8 True.
9 False: Wellington is the capital of New Zealand.
10 True.   (10 marks)

Test 26

26.1 1 e   2 d   3 b   4 j   5 h   6 c   7 f   8 a   9 i   10 g   (10 marks)

26.2
1 foggy   3 X   5 windy   7 snowy   9 X
2 sunny   4 thundery   6 X   8 rainy   10 cloudy
                                                            (10 marks)

26.3
1 Yesterday was a *sunny* day   4 a *thunderstorm*
2 and *foggy* in Chicago   5 raining and *windy*
3 It's very *dry*   (10 marks: 2 each)

Test 27

27.1 1 side   2 tell   3 get   4 near   5 on   (5 marks)

27.2
1 bus station   3 library   5 cash machine
2 bank   4 car park
                                                            (5 marks)

27.3
1 railway station   5 tourist information office   8 shopping centre
2 post office   6 No Smoking   9 town hall
3 Entrance; Exit   7 pedestrian area   10 car park
4 Out of order   (20 marks: 2 each)

Test 28

28.1 1 g   2 d   3 h   4 b   5 j   6 a   7 e   8 i   9 c   10 f   (10 marks)

28.2
1 village   3 forests   5 mountains   7 cottage   9 farm
2 path   4 river   6 lake/river   8 field   10 hills
                                                            (10 marks)

28.3
1 I love *nature*; a *conservation area* (2 marks)
2 we go *skiing*
3 a walk in *the country* / *the countryside*
4 There *is* some fantastic *wildlife*
5 in the *mountains*
6 a *city* in the *country* of Greece (2 marks)
7 the highest *mountain* in the world
8 go *for a walk* / *go walking*   (10 marks)

Test 29

29.1
1 snake   3 horse   5 giraffe   7 cow   9 monkey
2 elephant   4 tortoise   6 cat   8 parrot   10 rabbit/hare
                                                            (10 marks)

29.2
1 a foal
2 chicken
3 a zoo
4 eggs
5 wool
6 ham, pork, bacon (1 mark each for any two of these)
7 milk
8 a snake
9 leather   (10 marks)

29.3
1 Horse – because the others are all kinds of cats.
2 Snake – because the others have four legs and are mammals.
3 Sheep – because the others are all young/baby animals.
4 Pig – because the others are all pets. / Fish – because it lives in water and the others live on land.
5 Foal – because the others are all types of meat.

(10 marks: 1 for the word and 1 for the reason.
Note: there are other possible answers with different reasons.)

Test 30

30.1
1 bus		6 taxi	
2 boat		7 helicopter	
3 underground		8 ship/ferry	
4 (aero)plane		9 train	
5 motorbike/motorcycle		10 bicycle/bike	(10 marks)

30.2
1 a map / an atlas
2 your/a passport
3 the buffet/restaurant car
4 a single (ticket) / a one-way ticket
5 customs / a customs officer
6 luggage
7 a timetable
8 hire one / rent one
9 a boarding card
10 flight stewards / flight attendants / cabin attendants / cabin crew / cabin staff
(10 marks)

30.3   1 c   2 a   3 c   4 b   5 a   (10 marks: 2 each)

Test 31

31.1
1 Christmas
2 Bonfire Night
3 New Year's Eve
4 Hallowe'en
5 Valentine's Day   (10 marks: 2 each)

31.2

1	[Christmas	card]
2	bank	holiday
3	Yorkshire	pudding
4	royal	family
5	primary	school
6	roast	potatoes
7	Prime	Minister
8	Easter	eggs
9	Christmas	tree
10	Houses of	Parliament
11	chicken tikka	masala

Christmas pudding and *Easter card* are also possible combinations.

(10 marks)

31.3

Types of school	Hot things	People
nursery	[bonfire]	king
private	curry	Prime Minister
secondary	fireworks	queen
state	oven	

(5 marks: ½ for each word in the right column)

31.4
1 Valentine's Day
2 Bonfire Night
3 (roast) beef
4 chips
5 India

(5 marks)

Test 32

32.1

1 murder		5 steal		9 burglary	
2 mug		6 robbery		10 dealer	
3 terrorism / terrorist attack		7 robber			
4 car thief		8 shoplifter		(10 marks)	

32.2
1 burglary; broke; stole/took   4 robbed; robbers
2 murdered; murderer/killer   5 mugged/robbed
3 Shoplifting; shoplifters/thieves   6 thief; thefts / car thefts   (12 marks)

32.3
1 True
2 False: you have to pay a *fine*.
3 False: we call them *vandals*.
4 True.
5 True.
6 False: we call it a *court*.
7 False: we call it a prison.
8 True.

(8 marks)

Test 33

33.1 [1 c]   2 k   3 e   4 f   5 d   6 a   7 j   8 b   9 g   10 h   11 i

(10 marks)

33.2

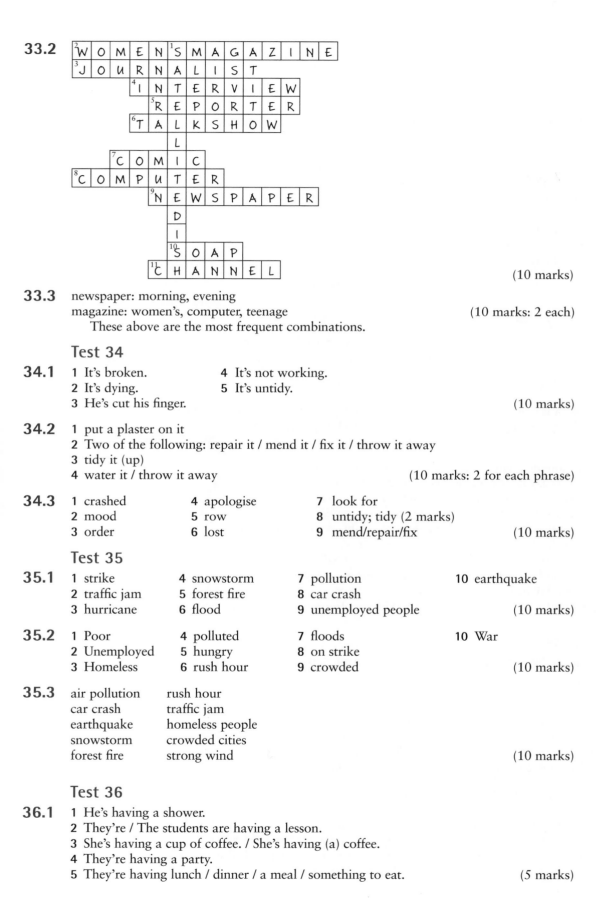

(10 marks)

33.3 newspaper: morning, evening
magazine: women's, computer, teenage   (10 marks: 2 each)
    These above are the most frequent combinations.

Test 34

34.1
1 It's broken.		4 It's not working.
2 It's dying.		5 It's untidy.
3 He's cut his finger.		(10 marks)

34.2
1 put a plaster on it
2 Two of the following: repair it / mend it / fix it / throw it away
3 tidy it (up)
4 water it / throw it away   (10 marks: 2 for each phrase)

34.3
1 crashed	4 apologise	7 look for
2 mood	5 row	8 untidy; tidy (2 marks)
3 order	6 lost	9 mend/repair/fix (10 marks)

Test 35

35.1
1 strike	4 snowstorm	7 pollution	10 earthquake
2 traffic jam	5 forest fire	8 car crash	
3 hurricane	6 flood	9 unemployed people	(10 marks)

35.2
1 Poor	4 polluted	7 floods	10 War
2 Unemployed	5 hungry	8 on strike	
3 Homeless	6 rush hour	9 crowded	(10 marks)

35.3
air pollution	rush hour
car crash	traffic jam
earthquake	homeless people
snowstorm	crowded cities
forest fire	strong wind (10 marks)

Test 36

36.1
1 He's having a shower.
2 They're / The students are having a lesson.
3 She's having a cup of coffee. / She's having (a) coffee.
4 They're having a party.
5 They're having lunch / dinner / a meal / something to eat.   (5 marks)

36.2   1 d   2 c   3 a   4 e   5 b   (5 marks)

36.3   1 hadn't (had not) got / didn't have; had to
          2 had
          3 Have … got; have
          4 has (got) to; have (got); have (got) to
          5 have
          6 had   (10 marks)

Possible answers:

36.4   1 Have a good journey!
          2 Can I have a go?
          3 Can I have a look?
          4 Have a good time!
          5 Can I have a word with you?   (5 marks)

36.5   1 meal   **2** meeting   **3** lesson   **4** homework; exam   (5 marks)

Test 37

37.1   1 by   3 away   5 up; down   7 back
          2 out of; into/onto   4 up   6 by   8 to   (10 marks)

37.2   1 c   2 a   3 b   4 c   5 b   (5 marks)

37.3   1 Nora is going shopping.   **4** Terry and Sarah are going sightseeing.
          2 Harry is going swimming.   **5** Nick is going fishing.
          3 Mel and Bob are going dancing.   (5 marks)

37.4   On Monday evening Jim is going to meet Tom and Ricky.
          On Tuesday he is going to visit his grandmother.
          On Wednesday he is going to meet Pat for dinner.
          On Thursday morning he is going to go swimming.
          On Thursday evening he is going to play table tennis with Mary.
          On Friday he is going to do some housework.
          On Friday he is also going to phone his Aunt Sally.
          On Saturday he is going to buy Tom's birthday present.
          On Sunday he is going to give Tom his present.
          On Sunday he is also going to take Mary to Tom's party.   (10 marks)

Test 38

38.1   1 done; did   2 Does; doesn't; does   3 Did; did; didn't   4 do; done

                                                                                   (10 marks)

38.2   1 What do you do?
          2 What do you do at the weekends?
          3 Let me do the washing-up / Let me do the dishes.
          4 I always do the/my housework/cleaning on Saturdays.
          5 I did my best / a lot of work but I failed / didn't pass the exam.   (5 marks)

38.3   1 MICHAEL: What *does* your father *do*?
                JANE: He's a lorry driver.
          2 I don't like *doing* homework but I know I have to *do it*.
          3 He *does* a lot of business with companies in the USA nowadays.
          4 I saw her at the gym. She *was doing* some exercises that looked very hard.
          5   DIANA: Liz, what *are you doing* with all those clothes?

LIZ: *I'm doing* my washing. All my clothes are dirty.

6 FATHER: Ivan, *do* your homework now!
    IVAN: No. Not now. *I'll do* it later. Please, Dad!
    FATHER: No! I want you *to do* it now!

7 MARIA: I *do* my best to learn all the new words every day.
    ANONA: So *do* I, but then I forget them again.

8 In our family, my father *does* the washing-up every day, my mother *does* the gardening, but my brother never *does* anything! (15 marks)

Test 39

39.1 1 Pam is making (some / a cup of) tea.
    2 Tim is making a photocopy.
    3 Rose is making a choice.
    4 Chris is making a video/film.
    5 Isabelle is making a mess.
    6 Phil is making an appointment (with the dentist).
    7 Sophie is making a mistake.
    8 Vincent is making dinner / lunch / a meal.
    9 Katy is making a/her/the bed.
    10 Nathan is making (some / a cup of) coffee. (10 marks)

39.2 do: your homework, an exam, the washing, the cooking, some exercises, the housework
make: [lunch], a noise, an appointment, a mistake, a choice (10 marks)

39.3 I did it very quickly, so I think I probably *made* a lot of mistakes. Then my friend and I went to a film. The hero died, so it made us feel very *sad/unhappy*. But it was a very long film, so it made *me* feel quite tired too. When I got home I had to *do* the washing. Then at last I could go to bed.
I've got to *take/do* an exam next week, but let's meet at the weekend.

(10 marks: 1 for identifying each mistake and 1 for each correction)

Test 40

40.1 1 coming home   4 comes from
    2 come here   5 come back
    3 coming out of (5 marks)

40.2 1 c   2 e   3 a   4 b   5 d (5 marks)

40.3 1 LORNA: Has your brother come back *from* Germany yet?
    JAMES: Yes, he *came home* last Friday.

2 HILDA: Do you know Stockholm? I've never been there.
    RYAN: Yes, I *went* there last summer for a few days.

3 STEVE: What nationality is Tanya? Where *does she come* from?
    FELIX: She *comes* from Moscow. She's Russian.

4 ANNA: I was surprised to see Julia in your office.
    NANCY: Yes, she didn't even knock. She just came *in*.

5 EVA: Do you know what the English word 'cabbage' means?
    PACO: Yes, it came *up* in the lesson yesterday. It's a vegetable.

6 ADA: Would you like to *come* round to my house this evening to watch a DVD?
    NIK: Yes, but my cousin is staying with me. Can he come *along*?
    ADA: Of course. He can *come* too.

(20 marks: 2 for each corrected mistake)

Test 41

41.1 1 It took Miranda an/one hour to go/get to work.
2 It took Tony twenty minutes to check his emails.
3 It took Maggie an hour and a quarter / an hour and fifteen minutes to do her homework.
4 It took Jeremy an hour and a half / an hour and thirty minutes / ninety minutes to fly/get to Paris.
5 It took Julia ten minutes to eat (her) lunch.
6 It took Mark two and a half hours to write a report.
7 It took Angela three hours forty minutes to go/get to London.
8 It took Paul three and a half hours to repair his bike.
9 It took Rosemary three months to write a story.
10 It took Ken eight years to write a poem.   (10 marks)

41.2 1 I took the train when I went to the airport last summer.
2 Anita is taking an English exam tomorrow. / Anita is going to take an English exam tomorrow.
3 Kay wants to take (some) Greek lessons.
4 Her father takes / took / is taking the bus to the office.
5 Pete takes the underground to work every day.

(10 marks: 2 for each sentence.
Give yourself 1 mark if you have just
one mistake in the sentence.)

41.3 a scarf   b money   c [umbrella]   d camera   e book   f apple
1 book   2 apple   3 camera   4 money   5 scarf   (10 marks: 1 for labelling
each picture, 1 for completing
each sentence)

Test 42

42.1 1 brings   2 taking   3 brought   4 bring   5 Take
(10 marks: 1 for each correct choice of *take*
or *bring*, 1 for each correct verb form)

These are suggested answers. Yours may be a little different, but you must choose the correct verb, *take* or *bring*, to get the marks.

42.2 1 I'll take / I can take / Let me take you to the station. / Do you want me to take you to the station?*
*If you are learning English in Ireland you may hear people saying *bring* here instead of *take*.
2 Will/would/can/could you take this parcel to the post office for me, please?
3 Would you like to come to our/my party and bring your guitar?
4 I'm going to take it back and change it / get a different size / get the right size.
5 Will/would/can/could you bring me back some Belgian chocolates?   (10 marks)

42.3

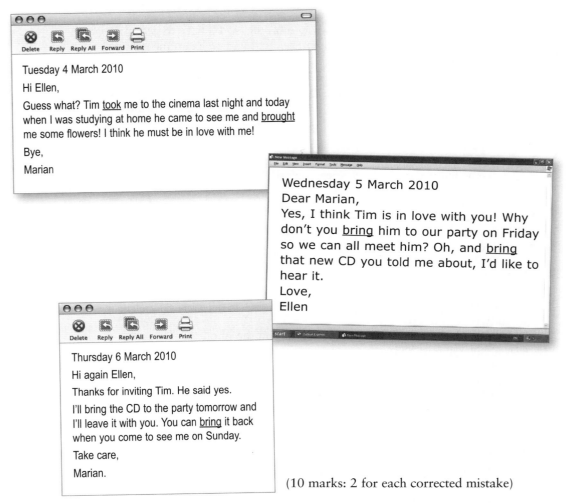

Tuesday 4 March 2010

Hi Ellen,

Guess what? Tim <u>took</u> me to the cinema last night and today when I was studying at home he came to see me and <u>brought</u> me some flowers! I think he must be in love with me!

Bye,

Marian

Wednesday 5 March 2010

Dear Marian,

Yes, I think Tim is in love with you! Why don't you <u>bring</u> him to our party on Friday so we can all meet him? Oh, and <u>bring</u> that new CD you told me about, I'd like to hear it.

Love,

Ellen

Thursday 6 March 2010

Hi again Ellen,

Thanks for inviting Tim. He said yes.

I'll bring the CD to the party tomorrow and I'll leave it with you. You can <u>bring</u> it back when you come to see me on Sunday.

Take care,

Marian.

(10 marks: 2 for each corrected mistake)

Test 43

43.1
1 warm(er)	5 thin(ner)/slim(mer)	9 cards/presents
2 interesting/exciting	6 ticket	10 emails/messages
3 shorter	7 money/cash	
4 rich(er)	8 bread/cakes	(10 marks)

43.2
1 When do/did you get to the station?
2 What time did you get to the theatre yesterday?
3 How do I get to the cinema?
4 When did/does your brother get to the airport on Monday?
5 How do I get to the restaurant?
(10 marks: 1 for writing questions with *get to* correctly and 1 for the correct place)

43.3
1 are getting	3 to get	5 is getting better	7 get to	9 get a newspaper
2 got married	4 gets home	6 get a job	8 got back/home	10 getting

(10 marks)

Test 44

44.1
1 turn	3 go	5 Get	7 put	9 turn
2 go	4 up	6 turn	8 Come / Go	10 take (10 marks)

44.2
1 d	3 e	5 b
2 c	4 a	(10 marks)

44.3 1 I have to get the train at 7.30 tomorrow morning, so I'll have to *get* up early.
2 I went *on* working until after midnight because I had an exam the next day.
3 It's raining; put *on* your raincoat.
4 They offered her the job but she turned it *down*.
5 If you *get* off the bus at Histon Street, you will see the museum on your left.
(10 marks: 2 for each corrected mistake)

Test 45

45.1 1 gets up   4 has breakfast
2 goes to the bathroom   5 goes to work
3 has a shower   (5 marks)

45.2 1 comes home   4 watches TV
2 makes dinner   5 goes to bed
3 has dinner   (5 marks)

45.3 1 Andy is watching TV.
2 Andy is having (his) breakfast.
3 Andy is making dinner / cooking.
4 Andy is getting up.
5 Andy is phoning/calling a friend / talking on the phone.
6 Andy is going to bed.
7 Andy is having dinner /eating.
8 Andy is going home / driving home / going to work / driving to work.
9 Andy is coming/arriving/getting home.
10 Andy is waking up.   (10 marks)

45.4 1 What time do you go to work?
2 How often do you clean the house?
3 What time do you (usually) get up?
4 How often do you go for a walk?
5 How often do you wash your clothes?
6 What time do you (usually) go to bed?
7 How often do you go to the supermarket?
8 What time do you (usually) come home?
9 How often do you go to your friend's house?
10 How often do you write a letter to your grandmother?   (10 marks)

Test 46

46.1 1 b   2 a   3 d   4 e   5 c   (5 marks)
(Note: 1e, 3e, 4b, 4c, 5b, 5c and 5e are also possible.)

46.2 1 say   2 told   3 say   4 tell   5 tell   (5 marks)

46.3 *Possible answers*:

1 Ask somebody the way. / Ask somebody how to get there. / Ask for directions.
2 Ask somebody the time. / Ask somebody what the time is. / Ask somebody what time it is. / Ask somebody if they have (got) the time.
3 Ask the teacher (to explain it). / Ask another student to help you. / Ask for a dictionary.
4 Ask (the waiter) for the bill.
5 Ask them to turn it down / turn it off.   (10 marks)

46.4
1 Will you *answer* it
2 she *speaks* excellent Danish
3 he hasn't *replied (to it) / answered it / written back* yet
4 How *do you say* 'Milan' in Italian?
5 He *told* me an interesting story (10 marks: 2 for each corrected mistake)

Test 47

47.1
1 He's driving (a bus).   6 He's swimming.
2 He's riding (a horse).   7 She's dancing.
3 She's walking.   8 He's flying (a plane).
4 She's falling.   9 He's climbing (a tree).
5 She's jumping.   10 He's carrying a suitcase.   (10 marks)

47.2 1 b   2 c   3 a   4 b   5 b   6 c   7 b   8 c   9 a   10 c   (10 marks)

47.3
1 running; swimming; riding   4   catch
2 drive; fly   5   walk; carry
3 dancing   6   falling   (10 marks)

Test 48

48.1
1 paragraph   3 dialogue   5 noun   7 sentence   9 phrase
2 adverb   4 singular   6 adjective 8 preposition   10 plural
(20 marks: 2 each)

48.2
1 boys (*boy's* means 'something the boy has', for example *the boy's camera*; it can also be a contraction for *boy is* or *boy has*.)
2 an adjective (the adverb is *nicely*)
3 works
4 man
5 door
6 at
7 easily
8 *put* is a verb
9 children (the singular is *child*)
10 True

(10 marks)

Test 49

49.1
1 Before; because
2 If; and
3 or
4 also; but
5 After (*When* or *Before* would also be possible here.)
6 so
7 when   (10 marks)

49.2 1 b   2 c   3 a   4 c   5 b   (10 marks: 2 each)

49.3
I'm going to study abroad and I'm really looking forward to it.
I'm going to study abroad, so I will be away from home for three years.
I'm going to study abroad when I've finished secondary school.
I'm going to study abroad if I get good grades in my exams.
I'm going to study abroad because I want to learn more about other countries and cultures.
(10 marks: 2 each)

Test 50

50.1
1 June
2 December
3 August
4 January
5 July
6 October
7 February
8 September
9 April
10 November   (10 marks)

50.2 1 f   2 k   [3 g]   4 h   5 j   6 d   7 i   8 e   9 b   10 c   11 a   (10 marks)

50.3
1 after   4 in; in
2 in; in   5 before
3 at; on; on; for   6 in   (10 marks)

Test 51

51.1
1 o'clock
2 hours ago
3 for two hours / since two o'clock   (5 marks)

51.2
1 May   4 Bill is on holiday for two weeks / for a fortnight.
2 March   5 23 April
3 February   (5 marks)

51.3

(10 marks: *occasionally* and *now and then* are very similar, so give yourself the mark if you put them the other way round.)

51.4
1 never; always   4 not often; occasionally
2 now and then; often   5 Usually; sometimes
3 rarely; usually   (5 marks)

51.5
1 At; moment; twice   4 the past
2 in a; soon   5 the future
3 once; recently   (5 marks)

Test 52

52.1
back – front
beginning – end
bottom – top
here – there
left – right   (10 marks)

52.2
1 a dog	3 the number 1	5 a boy/child	7 In	9 At
2 a (suit)case	4 a tree	6 a house	8 On	10 In

(10 marks)

52.3
1 here	3 away	5 middle	7 there	9 everywhere
2 out	4 abroad	6 back	8 left	10 side

(10 marks)

Test 53

53.1

Opposites	
good	bad
fast	slow
quiet	loud
sad	happy
friendly	unfriendly

(10 marks)

53.2
1 fast	6 in a very unfriendly way
2 loudly	7 badly
3 quietly	8 quickly
4 well	9 sadly
5 slowly	10 in a friendly way

(10 marks)

53.3
1 The child is speaking very quietly.
2 Glen/He was acting strangely.
3 The accident happened suddenly.
4 Pippa/She passed it / the exam easily.
5 He finished the job quickly.

(10 marks: 1 mark for choosing the right adjective
and 1 for putting it into the adverb form)

Test 54

54.1
1 information	4 furniture
2 accommodation	5 luggage
3 weather	

(10 marks)

54.2

Countable	Uncountable
shoe	milk
apple	money
bus	rice
plate	bread
	butter
	traffic

(10 marks)

54.3
1 Is *this furniture* new? I haven't seen *it* before. (2 marks)
2 We had terrible weather (not 'a')
3 three large *loaves of bread*
4 some *advice*
5 The *traffic is* always very bad
6 The news *is* on TV in five minutes. Shall we watch *it*? (2 marks)
7 Rail *travel is* more interesting
8 a lot of *work*   (10 marks)

Test 55

55.1

Good	Bad
excellent	dreadful
great	horrible
lovely	terrible
marvellous	
nice	
perfect	
wonderful	

(10 marks: 1 each)

55.2

1 great	3 excellent	5 brilliant	7 perfect	9 fine
2 horrible	4 awful	6 lovely	8 good	10 awful

(10 marks)

55.3

1 Perfect	5 marvellous	9 great
2 terrible	6 Excellent	10 dreadful
3 Lovely	7 awful	
4 horrible	8 Wonderful	

(10 marks)

Test 56

56.1

Positive	Negative
kind	horrible
wonderful	unhappy
easy-going	stupid
lovely	difficult
	selfish
	naughty

(10 marks)

56.2

1 lovely	6 happy
2 horrible	7 intelligent
3 difficult	8 naughty
4 kind	9 well-behaved
5 wonderful	10 stupid

(10 marks)

56.3
kind – selfish
happy – unhappy
lovely – horrible
stupid – intelligent
easy-going – difficult   (10 marks)

Test 57

57.1 [1 f] 2 i 3 k 4 a 5 g 6 b 7 j 8 e 9 c 10 d 11 h (10 marks)

57.2
1 for	4 about (*of* is also possible)	7 for
2 to	5 at; at	8 at
3 of	6 to	9 in (10 marks)

57.3
1 apologise	3 wait	5 pay	7 come	9 afraid
2 good	4 listen	6 proud	8 belong	10 look

(10 marks)

Test 58

58.1
1 pre-war	4 resend	7 uncomfortable	10 unfinished
2 non-smoking	5 ex-girlfriend	8 retell	
3 half-price	6 unhappy	9 informal	(10 marks)

58.2
1 He is the *ex-president* of the club.
2 I prefer *non-alcoholic* drinks.
3 I think you should *rewrite* your essay.
4 He seems to be *unhappy* in his job.
5 The restaurant has *half-price* meals for children.
6 I don't like to give *unfinished* homework to my teacher.
7 The *pre-school* years are very important for little children.
8 It is *impossible* for anyone to live for 200 years.
9 You can wear *informal* clothes to the party.
10 This chair is *uncomfortable*.   (10 marks)

58.3
1 This machine is *unsafe*.	6 The lessons are very *informal*
2 something *incorrect*	7 Mike is my *ex-boss*.
3 It is *impossible*	8 smoking or *non-smoking* seat
4 *pre-exam* nerves	9 a *half-hour* drive
5 some *unread* books	10 I *readdressed* the letter (10 marks)

Test 59

59.1

Suffix	Meaning of suffix	Example
er, or	person	footballer, swimmer, actor, teacher
er, or	machine or thing	tin opener, pencil sharpener
less	without	endless, careless
ness	makes an abstract noun from an adjective	darkness, weakness
y	makes an adjective from a noun	snowy, cloudy, funny

(10 marks: 1 for each suffix and 1
for adding another example.
Check in a dictionary if you are not sure whether
the example you suggest is correct or not.)

59.2
1 a hairdryer
2 a swimmer
3 a bottle opener
4 a builder
5 a traveller
6 a writer
7 a cooker
8 a teacher
9 a pencil sharpener
10 a singer   (10 marks: 1 for each word)

59.3
1 happily – d   4 cooker – e
2 sunny – c   5 rainy – f
3 sandy – b

(10 marks: 1 for forming the correct word
and 1 for matching the phrase to the right picture)

Test 60

60.1 1 b   2 b   3 a   4 b   5 b   6 a   7 a   8 b   9 b   10 b   (10 marks)

60.2

Word	Same sound
1 quiet	diet
2 lose	shoes
3 quite	fight
4 felt	belt
5 loose	juice

(10 marks)

60.3
1 I *lent* her my pen
2 a really good *cook*
3 I *fell* down the stairs
4 *expecting* to fail
5 *borrow* your tennis racket
6 They *check* your age
7 said 'Good *afternoon*' (Note: You say 'Good evening' when you arrive at someone's house between 5 pm and about 8 pm. If you arrive between 12 pm and 5 pm you say 'Good afternoon'. You say 'Good night' when you leave someone's house (after about 9 pm).)
8 I *hope* I pass it with a good grade.
9 I was surprised that nobody *checked* my ID
10 Her new flat is *quite* big

(10 marks)

Personal diary

Test	Word	Translation	Points to remember	Related words

Phonemic symbols

Vowel sounds

Symbol	Examples		
/iː/	sleep	me	
/i/	happy	recipe	
/ɪ/	pin	dinner	
/ʊ/	foot	could	pull
/uː/	do	shoe	through
/e/	red	head	said
/ə/	arrive	father	colour
/ɜː/	turn	bird	work
/ɔː/	sort	thought	walk
/æ/	cat	black	
/ʌ/	sun	enough	wonder
/ɒ/	got	watch	sock
/ɑː/	part	heart	laugh
/eɪ/	name	late	aim
/aɪ/	my	idea	time
/ɔɪ/	boy	noise	
/eə/	pair	where	bear
/ɪə/	hear	beer	
/əʊ/	go	home	show
/aʊ/	out	cow	
/ʊə/	pure	fewer	

Consonant sounds

Symbol	Examples		
/p/	put		
/b/	book		
/t/	take		
/d/	dog		
/k/	car	kick	
/g/	go	guarantee	
/tʃ/	catch	church	
/dʒ/	age	lounge	
/f/	for	cough	
/v/	love	vehicle	
/θ/	thick	path	
/ð/	this	mother	
/s/	since	rice	
/z/	zoo	houses	
/ʃ/	shop	sugar	machine
/ʒ/	pleasure	usual	vision
/h/	hear	hotel	
/m/	make		
/n/	name	now	
/ŋ/	bring		
/l/	look	while	
/r/	road		
/j/	young		
/w/	wear		